P9-CJC-705

Literature & Thought

The Main Event

Perfection Learning

EDITORIAL DIRECTOR   Julie A. Schumacher

SENIOR EDITOR   Terry Ofner

EDITOR   Sherrie Voss Matthews

PERMISSIONS   Laura Pieper

REVIEWER   Larry Bargenquast

DESIGN AND PHOTO RESEARCH   William Seabright and Associates, Wilmette, Illinois

COVER ART SPORTS ASSEMBLY Jim Tsinganos

ACKNOWLEDGMENTS

"Analysis of Baseball" by May Swenson. Copyright © 1971 by May Swenson. Used with permission of the Literary Estate of May Swenson.

CALVIN AND HOBBES © 1990 Watterson. Reprinted with permission of UNIVERSAL PRESS SYNDICATE. All rights reserved.

"Challenge" by Samuel Hazo. Copyright © Samuel Hazo. Reprinted by permission of the author.

"The Decline of Sport" from *The Second Tree From The Corner* by E. B. White. Copyright © 1935, 1936, 1937, 1938, 1939, 1940, 1941, 1942, 1943, 1944, 1945, 1946, 1947, 1948, 1949, 1950, 1951, 1952, 1953, 1954 by E. B. White. Reprinted by permission of HarperCollins Publishers, Inc.

"The Defender" by Robert Lipsyte, from *Ultimate Sports* by Donald R. Gallo. Copyright © 1995 by Donald R. Gallo. Used by permission of Random House Children's Books, a division of Random House, Inc.

"Dying to Win" by Merrell Noden. Reprinted courtesy of *Sports Illustrated* magazine, August 8, 1994. Copyright © 1994 Time, Inc. All rights reserved.

"Granny Ed and the Lewisville Raiders" by Rae Rainey. From *Young World*, copyright © 1977 by Review Publishing Co. Used by permission of Children's Better Health Institute, Benjamin Franklin Literary & Medical Society, Inc., Indianapolis, Indiana.

"In the Pocket" from *The Eye-Beaters, Blood, Victory, Madness, Buckhead and Mercy* by James Dickey. Copyright © 1968, 1969, 1970 by James Dickey. Used by permission of Doubleday, a division of Random House, Inc.   CONTINUED ON PAGE 144

WHAT IS THE VALUE OF SPORT?

The question above is the *essential question* that you will consider as you read this book. The literature, activities, and organization of the book will lead you to think critically about this question and to develop a deeper understanding of why people watch and play sports.

To help you shape your answer to the broad essential question, you will read and respond to four sections, or clusters. Each cluster addresses a specific question and thinking skill.

CLUSTER ONE What is sport? **DEFINE**

CLUSTER TWO What does it mean to be an athlete? **ANALYZE**

CLUSTER THREE Is winning everything? **INFER**

CLUSTER FOUR Thinking on your own **SYNTHESIZE**

Notice that the final cluster asks you to think independently about your answer to the essential question—*What is the value of sport?*

THE MAIN EVENT

NINE TRIADS

Three grand arcs:
the lift of the pole vaulter over the bar
the golf ball's flight to the green
the home run into the bleachers

Three pleasurable curves:
the ice skater's figure eight
the long cast of the fisherman
the arched back of the gymnast

Three swishes that lift the heart:
the basketball's spin through the net
the skier's swoop down the snowpacked hill
the diver's entry into the water

Three glides of satisfaction:
the ice hockey forward's, after the goal
the swimmer's turn at the end of the pool
the finish of the bobsled run

Three swift arrivals to admire:
the completed pass
the arrow into the bull's-eye
the sprinter at the tape

Three shots requiring skill:
the slapshot
the shot-put
the put-out

Three carriers of suspense:
the place kick for a field goal
the rim shot
three balls and two strikes

Three vital sounds:
the hunter's horn
the starter's gun
the bell for the end of the round

Three excellent wishes:
to move the body with grace
to fly without a machine
to outrun time

LILLIAN MORRISON

TABLE OF CONTENTS

FRIENDLY COMPETITORS:
A SPORTING CHANCE

Serious sport has nothing to do with fair play," wrote the British author George Orwell. "It is bound up with hatred, jealousy, boastfulness, disregard of all rules, and sadistic pleasure in witnessing violence."

Of course, sports enthusiasts are sure to disagree with Orwell. They will insist that fair play is, indeed, what sports are all about. After all, the word "sportsmanship" has come to signify some of the noblest qualities of the human spirit. These include grace in defeat, generosity in victory, and respect for one's opponent.

"Friendly competition," many people call it. But does this catchphrase really make sense? Isn't "friendly competition" a bit of a contradiction in terms?

Many of today's sports show telltale signs of a violent ancestry. In soccer, rugby, and American-style football, teams of players vie for territory in a manner suggestive of warfare. And can there be any doubt that wrestling and boxing are descended from more lethal forms of one-on-one combat?

How completely have such sports subdued their violent origins? The rules of football are periodically revised to keep players from causing one another harm, but players are routinely injured anyway. And boxing, praised for its emphasis on speed, grace, and skill, sometimes results in brain damage and death.

Even sports in which competitors make no physical contact can prove dangerous. In their determination to win at any cost, runners and gymnasts sometimes subject themselves to brutal regimens, dangerous substances, and unhealthy diets.

Indeed, the world of sports shows its dark side all too often. Brawls erupt among the players on the field, riots among the spectators in the stands. "I went to a fight the other day," a standup comedian once remarked, "and a hockey game broke out!"

So when we talk about friendly competition, are we only kidding ourselves? Does sportsmanship merely disguise destructiveness and aggression? Happily, many great stories from myth and folklore hint otherwise.

According to ancient Babylonian myth, King Gilgamesh of Uruk was a cruel king who caused his subjects untold misery. Then one day, a savage named Enkidu came from the forest and challenged the mighty Gilgamesh to a wrestling match. Although Gilgamesh narrowly won, he was so humbled by his opponent's valor and prowess that he became a wise and caring ruler. And he and Enkidu remained inseparable friends.

There is a similar legend about the fabled outlaw Robin Hood. In Sherwood Forest, Robin once met a burly stranger who challenged him to a fight. This time, the stranger won, knocking Robin headlong into a stream. Robin then befriended the stranger, nicknaming him "Little John."

And classical mythology tells of the beautiful, swift-footed huntress Atalanta, who refused to marry any man who couldn't outrun her in a race. She remained undefeated until a young man named Hippomenes challenged her. He won the race by dropping golden apples in Atalanta's path, distracting her attention. Atalanta happily married him. (Sports purists may object to Hippomenes' tactics. But the race, as they say, is not always to the swift—and Atalanta herself seems to have admired Hippomenes' cleverness.)

Gilgamesh, Robin Hood, and Atalanta all learned something about their own strengths and limitations from their challengers. Robin Hood and Atalanta could have skulked away bitterly in defeat, and Gilgamesh could have killed the defeated Enkidu. Instead, they had the good sense to befriend their challengers—the very people most able to keep them up to the mark. Friendly competition might not always be a reality in sports. But it is always an option. All it needs is a sporting chance.

SPORTS HALL OF FAME

Michael Jordan "His Airness" 1963- Chicago Bulls shooting guard, considered the best basketball player of all time. Played on two winning Olympic basketball teams, he also led the Bulls to six NBA championships.

Babe Didrikson Zaharias 1914-1956 Known as the best female all-around athlete of her time, she won three medals at the 1932 Olympics. She also won the women's U.S. Open golf tournament three times.

Florence Griffith Joyner "FloJo" 1959-1998 Three-time Olympian at the 1988 Olympics. She set records in the 100 meters (10.49 seconds) and the 200 meters (21.70).

Johnny Unitas 1933- Won four National Football League Championships for the Baltimore Colts, and threw touchdown passes in a record 47 consecutive games.

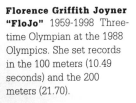

Nadia Comaneci
1961- Romanian gymnast who scored the first perfect 10 in competition at the 1976 Olympics for her flawless routine on the uneven parallel bars.

Pele 1940- Charismatic international ambassador of soccer. He led the Brazilian team to win three World Cups.

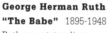

George Herman Ruth "The Babe" 1895-1948 Both an outstanding pitcher and outfielder, he set the record for most single season home runs in 1927 and set the record for most career home runs. Both lasted for decades.

Secretariat "Big Red"
1970-1985 Won horse racing's Triple Crown (Kentucky Derby, Belmont Stakes, Preakness Stakes) in 1973. Secretariat won the Belmont Stakes by a commanding 23 lengths.

Wayne Gretzky
"The Great One" 1961-
Hockey legend for his phenomenal scoring abilities, he lead the Edmonton Oilers to three Stanley Cups during the 1980s. He was voted the Most Valuable Player nine times and scored a record 92 goals during one season.

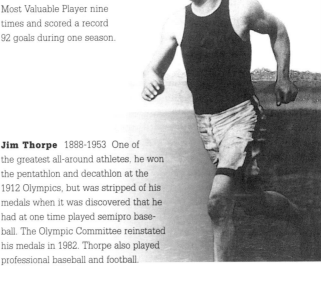

Jim Thorpe 1888-1953 One of the greatest all-around athletes, he won the pentathlon and decathlon at the 1912 Olympics, but was stripped of his medals when it was discovered that he had at one time played semipro base-ball. The Olympic Committee reinstated his medals in 1982. Thorpe also played professional baseball and football.

Martina Navratilova 1956-
Czech tennis player who dominated women's tennis from 1975-1994. She won 31 Grand Slam tournaments, and a record 167 titles during her career.

**Muhammad Ali
(Cassius Clay)
"The Greatest"** 1942-
After winning the 1960 Olympic gold in the light-heavyweight category, Ali went on to win the professional heavyweight title. He was stripped of the title in 1967 for refusing to fight in the Vietnam War. His title was reinstated in 1970; he went on to maintain his domi-nance in the sport until his retirement. He is now an advocate for victims of Parkinson's Disease, from which he suffers.

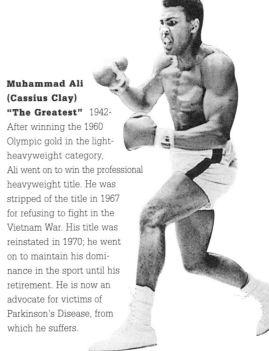

CONCEPT VOCABULARY

You will find the following terms and definitions useful as you read and discuss the selections in this book.

amateur athlete who engages in sport as a pastime rather than a profession

athlete a person trained in a sport or game requiring physical strength, agility, or stamina

athleticism characteristics of an athlete—vigorous, strong, fair-minded

camaraderie spirit of friendly fellowship

competition a contest between teams or individuals

competitor one who participates in a contest

courage mental or moral strength to perservere and withstand danger, fear, or difficulty

determination acting in a firm manner

hubris exaggerated pride or self-confidence

professional athlete who participates in a sport for money or as a career

sore loser athlete who does not lose gracefully

sport a source of diversion, recreation, and play

sportsmanship fairness, respect for one's opponent, and graciousness in winning and losing

teamwork work done by several athletes with each playing a specific part and playing to the benefit of the group

will mental power used to wish or intend a specific outcome

CLUSTER ONE

What Is Sport?

Thinking Skill   DEFINING

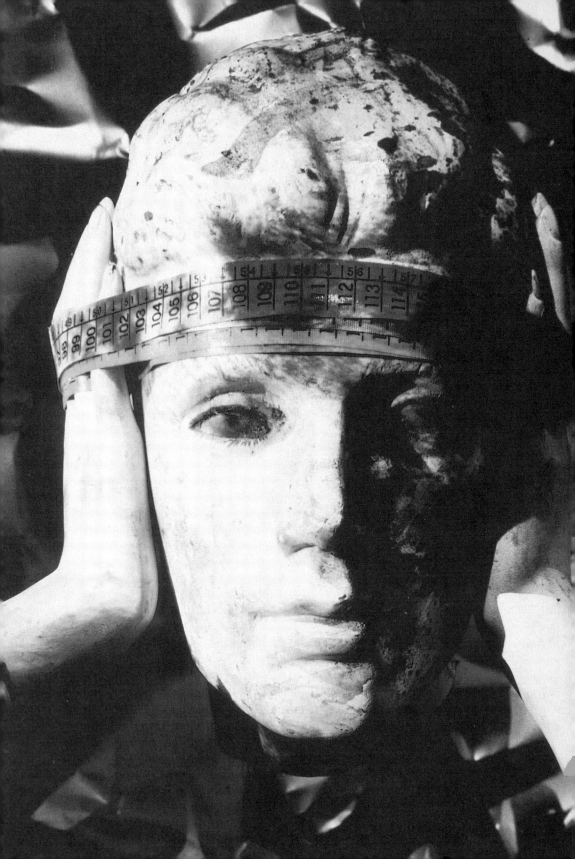

THE DEFENDER

ROBERT LIPSYTE

The Interscholastic Galactic Defender was licked awake by ice blue energy rays. Coach gently rocked his floating sleep slab. "Perfect day for the match, No. 1. Low humidity, no sunspots."

Coach tipped the slab and the Defender slid to the floor. He stepped out of his paper pajamas and onto the cleansing pedestal. A million beams refreshed his body, scraped his teeth, washed his hair, shaved his chin. The Defender then wrapped himself in a tunic of blue and gold, the school colors.

The Varsity was already at the training table. The Defender felt their admiration and envy as he took the empty seat at the head of the table.

He felt calm. His last high-school match. Across the table, his best friend, No. 2, winked. Good old No. 2, strong and steady. They had worked their way up the rankings ladder together since Basic School, rivals and teammates and buddies. It was almost over and he should have felt sad, but he didn't. One more match and he could be free to—

No. 4 caught his eye. He sensed that her feelings were the same. One more match and they wouldn't be numbers anymore, they would be Sophia and José, and they wouldn't have to guard their thoughts, or worse, turn them into darts and bombs.

Coach lifted a blue and gold competition thought helmet out of its recharging box and eased it down over the Defender's head. He fastened the chin strap, lengthened the antennae, and spun the dial to the lowest reception and projection power, just strong enough for noncompetitive thought in a small room.

For a moment, the Defender's mind was filled with a quivering cross-current of thought waves. There was a nasty pinprick from No. 7, only a sophomore but one of the toughest competitors in the galaxy, a star someday if he didn't burn himself out. There was a soothing velvet compress from No. 4, a hearty shoulder-banger from old No. 2.

The Defender cleared his mind for Coach, who was pacing the room. Psych talk time.

"As you know, the competition today, the Unified High School of the Barren Planets, is the first non-Earth team to ever reach the Galactic Finals. It wasn't expected and our scouting reports are incomplete."

No. 7 thought a blue and gold fireball wrecking the barren planets.

"Overconfidence can beat you," snapped Coach. "These guys are tough—kids from the orphan ships, the prison planets, the pioneer systems. They've lived through things you've only screened."

The freshperson substitute, No. 8, thought, "What about their Greenie No. 1?"

"We don't use the word 'Greenie,' " said Coach. "It's a bias word."

"A Greenie?" sneered No. 7. "A hairy little round Greenie?"

"Don't judge a mind by its body," snapped No. 4, blushing when she saw the Defender's approving blinks.

No. 7 leaned back and flashed an image of himself wearing hairy green bedroom slippers. Only No. 8 laughed.

Coach said, "We respect the Challenger. It wouldn't be here if it wasn't good."

" 'It'?" asked No. 2. "Male or female? Or a mixed gender?"

"We don't know anything about it," said Coach. "Except it's beaten everybody."

In silence, they drank their pregame meal—liquid fish protein and supercomplex carbs.[1]

Back on his slab, the Defender allowed his mind to wander. He usually spent his prematch meditation period reviewing the personality of his opponent—the character flaws, the gaps in understanding that would leave one vulnerable to a lightning thought jab, a volley of powerful images. But he knew nothing about today's opponent and little about Homo Vulgaris, mutant humans who had been treated badly ever since they began to appear after a nuclear accident. They were supposed to be stupid and unstable, one step above space ape. That one of them could

1 **carbs:** carbohydrates

actually have become No. 1 on the Power Thought Team of a major galactic high school was truly amazing. Either this one was very special, the Defender thought, or Earthlings hadn't heard the truth about these people.

He closed his eyes. He had thought he would be sentimental on the day of his last match, trying to remember every little detail. But he wished it were already over.

The wall-lights glowed yellow and he rose, dialing his helmet up to the warm-up level. He slipped into his competition robe. He began to flex his mind—logic exercises, picture bursts—as the elevator rose up through the Mental Athletics Department. When he waved to the chess team they stopped the clock to pound their kings on their boards in salute. The cyberspellers hand-signed cheers at him.

Officials were in the locker room running brain scans. The slightest trace of smart pills would mean instant disqualification. Everyone passed.

The Defender sat down next to No. 2. "We're almost there, Tombo." He flashed an image of the two of them lying in a meadow, smelling flowers.

Tombo laughed and bounced the image back, adding Sophia and his own girlfriend, Annie, to the meadow scene.

"Think sharp!" shouted Coach, and they lined up behind him in numerical order, keeping their minds blank as they trotted out into the roaring stadium. The Defender tipped his antennae toward his mother and father. He shook the Principal's hand.

"This is the most important moment of your life, No. 1. For the good of humanity, don't let those Unified mongrels outthink you."

The varsity teams from the Physical Athletics Department paraded by, four-hundred-pound football players and eight-foot basketball players and soccer players who moved on all fours. Some fans laughed at youngsters who needed to use their bodies to play. The Defender was always amazed at his grandfather's stories of the old days when the captain of the football team was a school hero.

It was in his father's time that cameras were invented to pick up brain waves and project them onto video screens for hundreds of thousands of fans in the arenas and millions more at home. Suddenly, kids who could think hard became more popular than kids who could hit hard.

"Let's go," roared Coach, and the first doubles team moved down into the Brain Pit.

The first match didn't last long. No. 7 and No. 4, even though they rarely spoke off the field, had been winning partners for three years. No. 7 swaggered to the midline of the court, arrogantly spinning his antennae, while No. 4 pressed her frail shoulders against the back wall. The Unified backcourter was a human female, but the frontcourter was a transspecies, a part-human lab creature ten feet tall and round as a cylinder.

The Defender sensed the steely tension in the Unified backcourter's mind; she was set for a hellfire smash. He was proud of No. 4's first serve, a soft, curling thought of autumn smoke and hushed country lanes, an ancient thought filled with breeze-riffled lily ponds and the smell of fresh-cut hay.

Off-balance, the backcourter sent it back weakly, and No. 7 filled the lovely image with the stench of backpack rockets, war gases, and kill zone wastes and fireballed it back. The Unified brainies were still wrestling with the image when the ref tapped the screamer. Too long. One point for the home team.

As usual, No. 7 lost points for unnecessary roughness—too much death and destruction without a logical lead-up to it—but as the fans cheered wildly he and No. 4 easily won. Their minds had hardly been stretched; the Psycho-Chem Docs in the Relaxant Room would need little tranquilspray to calm them down. Good, thought the Defender; No. 4 would be out in time for his match.

Except for thinking about her, the Defender began to lose interest in the day. How many times had he waited to go down into a Pit and attack another mind? It had seemed exciting four years ago when Coach had pulled him out of a freshperson mental gym class and asked him to try out for the team. His tests had shown mental agility, vivid imagery, and, most important, telepathic[2] potential.

It was the first thing he had ever been really good at. After he won a few matches, the popular kids began talking to him in the halls. Teachers asked him about the team. Letters began arriving at home from colleges owned by major corporations. His parents were so proud. He would be set for life.

But now it seemed like such a waste—fighting with thoughts instead of creating with them. Maybe he was just tired at the end of a long, tough season of defending his title. He thought about the meadow, with Sophia

---

2 **telepathic:** communication between minds using extrasensory means

and Tombo and Annie. Instead of thoughts, they would throw an ancient toy around. It was called something like frisbill. Frisboo? Frisbee!

Coach tapped his helmet. "Pay attention."

No. 5 and No. 6 were staggering under a vicious barrage. They lost, and the standings at the end of the doubles were even, 1–1.

The crowd fell silent as No. 3 lost her singles match and the scoreboard blinked Visitors 2, Home 1. As No. 2 lumbered down to the Pit, the Defender sent an image of a victory wreath to him.

Good old No. 2, steady and even-tempered and sure of himself. Mentally tough. He might have been No. 1 on any other high-school team, but he never showed resentment. For a moment, the Defender almost wished that No. 2 would lose; then the score would be 3–1 and nothing No. 1 could do would be able to salvage the team match. No pressure—he could play the game just for himself. If he won, great, he'd be the first player in history to win the championship twice. If he lost he would only disappoint himself; he wouldn't be letting his team and his school—and humanity, according to the Principal—down.

But No. 2 won and the score was tied and it was up to him.

The No. 1 player for the Unified High School of the Barren Planets, the Interscholastic Galactic Challenger, was waiting for him in the Pit.

He (she? it?) looked like a green teddy bear. The Defender had never seen one in the flesh. He forced his mind to think of the creature only as an opponent.

The Defender served first, a probing serve to test the quickness of the Challenger. He used an image, from a poet who had written in the dying language called English, of a youth gliding over a hilltop at night to catch a star falling from a shower of milk-white light.

The Challenger slapped it right back; the star was nothing but a burnt-out children's sparkler made from fuel wastes. The youth on the hilltop was left with a sticky purple mess.

The Defender was surprised at how long he struggled with the sadness of the thought. A Judge hit the screamer. Unified led, 1–0.

Coach called time-out.

The falling-star image had been one of his best serves, a frequent ace. No one had ever handled it so well, turning the beautiful vision of humanity's quest for immortality into an ugly image of self-destruction.

They decided to switch tactics—to serve a fireball, No. 7 style. The Defender hurled a blazing tornado of searing gases and immeasurable heat. The Challenger's mind scooped it up like a hockey puck and plopped it into an ocean filled with icebergs.

Off-balance, the Defender tried to give himself time by thinking steaming vapors from the ocean, but the Challenger turned the vapors into great fleecy clouds that shaped themselves into mocking caricatures[3] of famous Earthlings.

Desperately, the Defender answered with another fireball, and a Judge hit the screamer, calling it a Non Sequitur—the thought had not logically followed the Challenger's thought.

Unified led, 2–0.

The Defender served a complex image of universal peace: white-robed choruses in sweet harmony, endless vials of nutrient liquids flowing through galaxies aglow with life-giving stars, and hands—white, brown, green, orange, blue, black, red, and yellow—clasped.

The Challenger slashed back with mineral dredges that drowned out the singing, lasers that poisoned the vials, and a dark night created by monster Earth shields that were purposely blocking the sunlight of a small planet. The clasping hands tightened until they crushed each other to bloody pulp.

The Defender was gasping at the bitter overload when he heard the screamer. He was down, 3–0. He had never lost his serve before.

The Challenger's first serve was vividly simple: black Earthling trooper boots stomping on thousands of green forms like itself.

Screamer.

The Judge called "Foul" and explained that the thought was too political—the Galactic League was still debating whether Earth colonists had trampled the rights of the hairy green offspring of the accident victims.

The Challenger's second serve was an image of black-gloved Earthling hands pulling apart Greenie families and shoving parents and children into separate cages.

Foul screamer.

The third serve was an image of Earth rocket exhausts aimed to burn down Greenie houses.

Foul screamer.

Tie score, 3–3. The Judge called an official time-out.

---

3 **caricatures:** drawings with exaggerated features

Coach's strong thumbs were working under the Defender's helmet. "Register a protest, right now. Don't let that little fur ball make a farce of the game."

"He's allowed to think freely," said the Defender. He wondered if the Challenger was a "he." Did it matter?

"He's using the game just to further his cause."

"Maybe he has a just cause."

"Doesn't matter," said Coach. "This is a game."

"I'll get him next period," said the Defender, trying to sound more confident than he was.

The second period was a repeat of the first. The Defender's best serves were deflected, twisted, sent back in bewildering patterns while the Challenger fouled on three more images of Earthling inhumanity. As the scoreboard glowed 6–6, the crowd buzzed angrily.

Coach said, "I order you to register a protest or you will never play for this high school again."

"It's my last game here."

"I'll see you don't get a college scholarship."

"I'm not sure I ever want to play this game again."

"Look, José"—Coach's voice became soft, wheedling[4]—"you are the best high-school player who ever—"

"Not anymore," said the Defender.

His helmet had never felt so tight—it was crushing his mind numb—as he trudged out for the last regulation period.

His three serves were weak, random flashes of thought that barely registered on the video screens. The Challenger easily re-created them into bursting thoughts that made the Defender's head spin. The Challenger's three serves were cluster bombs of cruelty and greed, horrible images of his people trapped in starvation and hopelessness because of Earth. They were all called foul.

It was 9–9 going into sudden-death overtime.

The Principal was waiting for No. 1 at the edge of the Pit. With him was the Chief Judge, the Superintendent of Earth High Schools, the Commissioner of the Mental Athletics Association, the Secretary-General of the Galactic League, and other important-looking faces he recognized from telepathé-news.

---

4 **wheedling:** influencing by flattery

They all nodded as the Principal said, "You are the Defender. You have a responsibility to your school, your people, the planet. I order you to register a protest. We cannot be beaten by a foul little malcontent Greenie."

"It's only a game," said the Defender.

"Maybe to you," snapped the Superintendent.

He strode back into the Pit.

The Challenger had never left; the Defender suddenly realized the little creature had no coach or friends. He had come up alone to stand and fight for himself and his people.

The warning buzzer sounded. Seconds to serve. Sudden death. The Defender would go first. He thought of his all-time best serves, the ones he saved for desperate situations, because coming up with them was so exhausting, so mind-bending that if they failed he was lost. He thought of the end of the world, of sucking black holes, of nightmares beyond hope.

Suddenly he knew what to do.

He served an image of a dry and dusty field on a lonely colony planet. The land was scarred and barren, filled with thousands of round green creatures standing hopelessly beyond barbed wire as a harsh wind ruffled their dry fur.

For the first time, the Challenger took the full five seconds to return serve. He was obviously puzzled. His return was his weakest so far, merely widening the image to include a ring of Earthlings, healthy and happy, pointing and laughing at the Greenies. It was just what the Defender had expected.

He took his full five, then sent a soft, slow image of two Earthlings leaving the circle to walk among the Greenies until they picked one whose hands they held.

They led it skipping into a golden meadow under a sunny blue sky. The Earthlings were José and Sophia, and the Greenie who danced and sang with them was the Challenger.

In the shocked silence of the arena, the Challenger took the thought as if it were a knockout punch, his mind wobbling.

He was unable to deal with the thought, the kindness in it, the fellowship.

He can't handle love, thought the Defender. What a way to win.

The Challenger was still struggling to answer when the screamer sounded.

The match was over, 10–9. The crowd was roaring, the Principal was dancing on his chair, the video screens were filled with the face of José Nuñez, the first ever to win the galactic championship twice.

They swarmed around him now, the important faces, calling his name, slapping at his helmet, but he pushed through, shutting out their congratulations, the screams of the crowd, the exploding scoreboard.

He made his way through to the Challenger, alone and quivering in the middle of the Pit. I don't even know its name, thought the Defender. "It"?

Sophia and Tombo were running toward them. They knew what José was thinking.

It was only a game.

But it might be a start. ∾

WATCHING GYMNASTS

ROBERT FRANCIS

Competing not so much with one another
As with perfection
    They follow follow as voices in a fugue[1]
    A severe music.

Something difficult they are making clear
Like the crack teacher
    Demonstrating their paradigms[2] until
    The dumb see.

How flower-light they toss themselves,
    how light
They toss and fall
    And flower-light, precise, and arabesque[3]
    Let their praise be.

1 **fugue:** a musical composition where a phrase started by one instrument
is imitated and developed by others

2 **paradigm:** a clear example

3 **arabesque:** a posture in ballet where the body is bent forward from
the hip on one leg with one arm extended forward and the other arm
and leg extended backward; an intricate pattern

CHALLENGE

SAMUEL HAZO

Leveling his pole like some quixotic[1] lance,
trotting, trotting, faster, faster to his mark,
slotting the pole, twisting upward to a bar,
contortioning clear, the vaulter drops in sand.

He wipes his hands and stumbles from the pit
with sand still sweated to his thighs and calves,
retrieves the pole and drags it like a mast
behind him down the cinder aisle, and waits.

I feel in my onlooker's hands the taped
and heavy barrel of the vaulter's pole
and see the bar notched higher for his leap.
His spikes clench earth, and all my muscles pull
to face a task with nothing but my skill
and struggle for the mark I must excel.

1 **quixotic:** impractical; related to Don Quixote, who
attacked windmills with a lance

ANALYSIS OF BASEBALL

MAY SWENSON

It's about
the ball,
the bat,
and the mitt.
Ball hits
bat, or it
hits mitt.
Bat doesn't
hit ball, bat
meets it.
Ball bounces
off bat, flies
air, or thuds
ground (dud)
or it
fits mitt.

Bat waits
for ball
to mate.
Ball hates
to take bat's
bait. Ball
flirts, bat's
late, don't
keep the date.
Ball goes in
(thwack) to mitt,
and goes out
(thwack) back
to mitt.

Ball fits
mitt, but
not all
the time.
Sometimes
ball gets hit
(pow) when bat
meets it,
and sails
to a place
where mitt°
has to quit
in disgrace.
That's about
the bases
loaded,
about 40,000
fans exploded.

It's about
the ball,
the bat,
the mitt,
the bases°
and the fans.
It's done
on a diamond,
and for fun.
It's about
home, and it's
about run.

IN THE POCKET

JAMES DICKEY

NFL

Going backward
All of me and some
of my friends are forming a shell   my arm is looking
Everywhere and some are breaking
In   breaking down
And out   breaking
Across, and one is going deep   deeper
Than my arm. Where is Number One hooking
Into the violent green alive
With linebackers? I cannot find him he cannot beat
His man   I fall back more
Into the pocket   it is raging and breaking
Number Two has disappeared into the chalk
Of the sideline   Number Three is cutting with half
A step of grace   my friends are crumbling
Around me the wrong color
Is looming   hands are coming
Up and over between
My arm and Number Three: throw it hit him in the middle
Of his enemies   hit move scramble
Before death and the ground
Come up   LEAP STAND KILL DIE STRIKE

Now.

People have asked how to play Calvinball. It's pretty simple:
you make up the rules as you go. —BILL WATTERSON

The Olympics in Ancient Greece

Richard D. Burns/Diana falls

The Olympic Games gained their name from their birthplace, the Greek city of Olympia in the small "kingdom" of Elis. The first record we have of an Olympic Game being held is in the year 776 B.C. The first recorded champion was a fellow by the name of Coroebus, a cook, who lived in Elis. He had won the sprint from one end of the stadium to the other—one "stade" or about 180 meters (600 feet).

The Greeks later dated their calendar by this event. They also began keeping records of Olympic winners, often erecting statues to honor the most famous of champions. Finally, the Greeks began charting their history by Olympiads—the four-year cycle between the Games—a practice that would continue uninterrupted for more than a thousand years.

The earliest sporting activity at Olympia, as elsewhere in Greece, was a mixture of athleticism, religion, education, culture, and the arts. The contestants were local men from the surrounding cities and villages who came to the festivals to honor the gods and test themselves.

THE RISE OF THE GAMES

After the first dozen Games, the festival of Olympia came to include participants from more distant city-states. The Spartans, who emphasized the virtues of rigorous physical exercise, provided outstanding athletes, and dominated the Games.

DISCUS THROWER
c. 450 B.C.
Myron

Nothing was more important to the Greeks than the Games, not even their unceasing warring among themselves. Moved by the spiritual context of the Games, King Iphitus of Elis, supported by other rulers and legislators, agreed to stop all fighting for the duration of the Olympic Festival. This cessation of hostilities became known as the Olympic Truce.

Different sporting events were gradually introduced to the Games, including such activities as jumping, throwing, wrestling, boxing, and chariot racing. Running events, also, were expanded to include races of different lengths.

A TYPICAL OLYMPIC FESTIVAL

In the spring of an Olympic year, three sacred heralds would set out from Olympia to visit every corner of the Greek world and announce the forthcoming games.

Each Greek city-state sent its best men, determined by local elimination trials. The winner would be decorated with a simple branch of wild olive, but the rewards were great in other ways. The crowds idolized the great athletes, poets wrote odes to their triumphs, and sculptors immortalized them in bronze and marble. From the fifth century onward, monetary rewards also became associated with an Olympic championship.

Sitting in the scorching mid-summer heat, the male audience would witness an extraordinary variety of activities. There were all of the sporting events—running, jumping, throwing, equestrian,[1] and wrestling. In addition, there would be contests involving poetry, drama, and music.

Women were barred from the stadium, even as spectators, because the male athletes performed naked and because it would have been unthinkable for women to perform likewise. Young girls could watch the events taking place inside the stadium; but the only woman in the stadium was the priestess of Demeter, the goddess of agriculture, who was required to watch the Games from the north side of the stadium.

Penalties for women who violated this prohibition were supposed to be harsh; however, there is no record of a severe penalty being administered.

Apparently, only one woman, Kallipateira, daughter of Diagoras, was caught entering the stadium. She had trained her son Peisirodos in the skill of boxing and, on the day he fought in the Games, she slipped into the stadium disguised as a trainer. When her son won, she jumped over

1 **equestrian:** related to horseback riding

the barrier to embrace him and was recognized as a woman. The judges, because of her family's history of loyalty to the Games, were lenient and did not punish her. However, from then on the trainers also were required to appear nude.

Outside the stadium, southwards toward the wide river valley, was the hippodrome where chariot races were held. Women were allowed in the hippodrome and were victors of some equestrian events, as Olympic championships were awarded to the owners of the horses.

THE OPENING DAY'S EVENTS

At Olympia, the chariot race was the opening event, but only after a previous day of preparation and worship. The two-wheeled chariots, each drawn by four horses abreast, entered the stadium in a ceremonial procession led by judges dressed in purple robes, a herald, and a trumpeter. As each chariot passed in front of the judges' stand, the herald would call out the names of the owner, his father, and his city. Then he would proclaim that the games were officially open.

The number of chariots varied, up to 41 at the Pythian Games in 462 B.C. A large field made an exciting contest because they all would start together and rush toward the turning post some 400 meters away. The trumpeter would signal the start, and the chariots would make 12 laps, more than nine kilometers, around the turning post.

Chariot races were very dangerous and required the most skillful of drivers. Collisions were common on the narrow course, and it was not uncommon for only one chariot to complete the race. Not unlike modern times, it was the accidents that provided most of the thrills for the crowd.

THE SECOND DAY'S EVENTS

The pentathlon was held during the afternoon of the second day. The athletes had to participate in five events—the discus, the long jump, javelin, 200-meter sprint, and wrestling. All events except the final event, wrestling, were held in the stadium, while the wrestling took place in an open area near the altar of Zeus.

THE THIRD DAY'S EVENTS

The third day of competition was scheduled to coincide with the second or third full moon after the summer solstice.[2] The morning was dominated with religious activities. Varied religious rites, private and public, were followed by a great procession that began at the magistrate's house and wound its way to the altar of Zeus. The parade included judges, priests, the representatives from the cities, athletes, friends, and trainers. Arriving at the altar, they watched the slaying of 100 oxen. The roasted meat was taken to the magistrate's house where it was consumed at a gala[3] banquet.

During the afternoon, three events for boys were held—the 200-meter race, wrestling, and boxing. A "boy" was defined as a young male between the ages of 12 and 17. This rather loose definition in a society without birth certificates created some problems, but not enough to cause the creation of classes of boys, as was done in other Greek games.

THE FINAL DAY'S EVENTS

The morning of the final day was occupied with three running events—200 meters, 400 meters, and the long distance race ("Dolichos") of 4,800 meters. The 200-meter sprint was simply a full dash across the stadium, but the historical accounts of the longer runs have left us with some unanswered questions. Was there one turning pole for runners, or separate turning poles for each athlete? There were rules against tripping and bumping, but ancient writers suggest that such tricks were frequent.

Because they were run on the same day, only a truly extraordinary athlete could win all three sprinting events at the same Games. Such an individual would be called a tripler.

The greatest Olympic runner was Leonidas of Rhodes who won all three events at four consecutive Festivals spanning twelve years between 164 and 152 B.C. Another outstanding competitor was Polites of Keramos who won the two short sprints and the Dolichos in one day.

Finally, on the last afternoon came the rough but popular body contact sports: boxing, wrestling, and pancratium.[4]

2 **summer solstice:** June 22, when the earth is at its greatest distance from the sun

3 **gala:** festive celebration

4 **pancratium:** sport combining wresting and judo

The procedure was simple. Names were drawn from a silver urn setting up initial matches and creating the "pairing" of matches that would lead to the final or championship bouts. All three sports were brutal, with few rules, no time limits, and no ring. There were also no weight classes, so the competition was limited to big, tough, well-muscled men.

The objective in wrestling was to score three falls, a fall being defined as touching the ground with the knees. Milo of Croton was one of the most famous of the legendary strong men who won this popular event. He is said to have developed his great strength by carrying a calf around every day, and as the calf grew into a large bull, he would be carrying each day a heavier weight. There may have been some truth to this story, for Milo won the boys' wrestling in 540 B.C. and the senior event at five successive Games.

Presumably biting or gouging was prohibited, but not much else was. A fifth century B.C. wrestler named Leonticus, from Messina in Sicily, tried to break his opponent's fingers as quickly as possible. He was remembered as one of the first wrestlers to develop new "holds."

Boxing, however, was even more brutal than wrestling. Leather thongs were wound tightly around the hands and wrists, leaving the fingers free. Blows were allowed with the fist and hand. The two contestants fought

on without break until one or the other was knocked out or raised his hand as a sign of defeat. Violent activity was what attracted the spectators and that was what they saw.

The final pugilistic[5] event in the afternoon of the fourth day was the pancratium—a combination of wrestling and judo, with a bit of boxing thrown in. The contestants punched, slapped, kicked, wrestled, and, though illegal, would bite and gouge each other until one surrendered by tapping the victor on the back or shoulder.

One more event remained before the competition was closed, the 400-meter race in armor. Some writers say that it was held last to mark the end of the truce that was struck for each of the Games by warring states. The simpler and more plausible explanation is that it was felt desirable to reflect in the Games the fact that the infantry had supplanted the cavalry as the main Greek military unit.

THE EXPANSION OF ATHLETICS

Athletics reached a peak of popularity between the fifth and sixth centuries B.C. Almost 200 years after the first recorded festival at Olympia, other major sports festivals were established. The Pythian Games in honor of the god Apollo were begun at Delphi in 582 B.C. The Isthmian Games were begun near Corinth the same year, held in honor of the god Poseidon. With the addition of the Nemean Games, the fourth major festival was founded.

Not surprisingly, the greatest ambition of the Greek athlete was to win a championship at each of the Games. As the competition became more intense, the participants gradually changed. The first Olympic Games were dominated by the part-time, occasional local athletes from nearby villages, but as these Games began to grow in popularity they became dominated by young men of wealth who had the resources to hire the best coaches and the time to train.

However, as the sports circuit expanded many of the athletes became professionals who lived off the rewards bestowed by the state and aristocracy.[6] These young men trained year-round and traveled from festival to festival, including the Olympic Games, to compete with one another for the increasingly larger prizes.

---

5 **pugilistic:** boxing

6 **aristocracy:** government consisting of a small, privileged class, usually with ranks like king, queen, duke, duchess, lord, and lady

Among the major sports festivals, only the Olympic Games did not offer cash prizes. The glory of becoming an Olympic champion had a great many rewards—being honored in song, story, and victory parades. There were financial rewards as well, given by grateful cities and local wealthy sportsmen. When Olympic champions retired they could usually count on ample pensions to support them the rest of their lives.

THE DECLINE OF THE GAMES

The glory of the Olympic Games peaked at the height of classical Greek culture, some 250 years after the first recorded Games. Their decline was long and gradual, lasting some 950 years.

The first major blow to the Games came in 146 B.C. when they were moved to Rome after Greece was conquered and made part of the Roman Empire. Here the ideals of Olympia, the purity of the athletic contests, became less important. As the Games became entertainment spectacles, they took on unsavory overtones.

Some athletes began accepting money from opponents in exchange for conceding victory, in spite of the threat of extensive penalties. The Emperor Nero, for example, arranged for several Olympic crowns to be awarded to him after forcing his opponents to withdraw.

In Rome, as profit and politics came to dominate competition, the Olympic Games lost their historic and religious origins.

The final blow to the Games came with rise of early Christianity, which frowned upon glorification of the human body, viewed the celebration of Greek gods as a pagan[7] ritual, and disliked the brutality and corruption of the Games. The Christian Emperor Theodosius I banned all pagan festivals, including the Games, in A.D. 393. However, they continued to be held until the ban was reissued and enforced by Justinian I in A.D. 529. ∾

---

7 **pagan:** a follower of a religion that has multiple gods

RESPONDING TO CLUSTER ONE

WHAT IS SPORT?

Thinking Skill DEFINING

1. What does José mean at the end of "The Defender," when he says, "It was only a game. But it might be a start"?

2. Calvin has an interesting view of sports—the less organized the game, the better. Do you think that a sport has to be competitive to be fun? Be prepared to explain your answer.

3. **Imagery,** the use of words and phrases that appeal to the five senses, helps a writer convey maximum meaning with a minimum of words. Choose two poems from this cluster and record images that appeal to sight, sound, taste, touch, or smell.

4. List four ways in which sports today are the same as sports in ancient Greece and four ways in which they are different.

5. For each of the selections in this cluster, list two things that make the game a sport. The chart below will help you organize your ideas. Then use the information to write your own **definition** of sport.

Selection	Sport	What makes it a sport?
The Defender		
Calvinball		
Watching Gymnasts		
Challenge		
Analysis of Baseball		
In the Pocket		

Writing Activity: The Essence of Sport

Choose five of the activities below and use the **definition** you developed above to explain why each one is or is not a sport. Change your definition if you need to.

cheerleading	Monopoly	hunting	Rollerblading
NASCAR racing	skateboarding	mountain climbing	chess
skydiving	fishing	figure skating	Frisbee

For This Activity

• begin by stating your definition of sport

• then, describe each of the five activities and explain why it does or does not fit your definition

CLUSTER TWO

What Does It Mean to Be an Athlete?

Thinking Skill ANALYZING

THIS GIRL GETS
HER KICKS

RICK REILLY

Q: *How come nobody said a word last week after the Chatfield (Colo.)*
High homecoming queen accepted a single white rose at halftime of
the football game, locked arms with the king and then ripped off her
satin sash and sprinted into the players' locker room?
A: *She still had two quarters to play.*

Katie Hnida (pronounced NYE-duh) is 17, with long blond hair, melt-your-heart blue eyes, and legs that won't quit kicking. This season she's perfect: 23 for 23 on extra points, 3 for 3 on field goals and 1 for 1 in homecoming queen elections.

Among the best sports moments of the 1990s, this one has to be in the top 10: Katie tearing off her helmet at the end of the first half, taking her place among other members of the homecoming court in their dresses and high heels, being announced as queen, wriggling the sash on over her shoulder pads, waving thanks to everybody, smiling for the photographers and sprinting to the dressing room. "I only had a minute," she says of her coronation.

Is this a great time or what? We're past the 1970s, when girls had two options in sports: cheerleader or pep squad. We're past the '80s, when girls had two options in life: to be a jock or a girl. Now we're into the Katie Era, when a young lady can kick the winning field goal on Saturday

Katie Hnida during homecoming halftime.

afternoon and look drop-dead in her spaghetti-strap number on Saturday night. "I know I looked gross at halftime," Katie says. "No makeup or anything. But I'm a football player. How else am I going to look?"

Actually, the only way anyone on the other team can guess that the 5'9", 135-pound Katie is a girl is by the ponytail that runs out from beneath her helmet and down her back. One time, as a freshman, she got flattened after a PAT[1] by a massive nosetackle, who ended up on top of her. They both opened their eyes at the same time, only it was the nosetackle who screamed, "You're a girl!"

Not that the guys on the Chatfield High team seem to notice much. "I don't mind when they burp and spit around me," she says. "It lets me know they think of me as their teammate."

Another first: players thanked for impersonating water buffalo.

Katie's life can be strange. After one game last year the Chatfield players and their opponents were exchanging postgame handshakes when a hulk on the other team stopped Katie and asked, "Do you have another number besides 40 I could possibly have?" She didn't bite, but it still goes

1 **PAT:** point after touchdown

down as the single best pickup line in high school football history.

The only downside of the whole thing is that Katie has to shower and dress in the girls' locker room, away from the rest of the team. "Sometimes we'll win a big game and I can hear all the guys whooping it up," she says, "and I want to get in there with them."

Other than that, Katie "gets to be who she wants to be," says her mother, Anne, who never had that chance in high school. "I kept stats for the boys' basketball team," she says. Katie, meanwhile, has a 3.2 grade point average, writes and edits for the school newspaper, plays soccer in the spring, doesn't drink, won't smoke, can take a lick and kicks like a mule.

"Wearing a little skirt and jumping around after touchdowns isn't quite the same," she says. "I want the competition. I want to be part of the team. Girls ask me all the time, 'What's it like to be around all these gorgeous guys all the time?' They have no idea. I've seen these guys break down and cry in the huddle, and I've seen them so incredibly happy after a big win. I wouldn't trade anything for what I've had, being part of this team."

Yeah, she'd even trade the sash. "Ten years from now, nobody's going to be impressed that I was homecoming queen," she says, "but they might think it was cool I could kick a 40-yard field goal."

Katie, who has already booted a 35-yarder, has this crazy dream that would make things even cooler. She wants to become the only Division I woman football player next season. Colorado coach Rick Neuheisel already has asked her to walk on. Me, I'd bet my last pair of hose on her.

One thing, no guy's ever going to have to give Katie his letter jacket. She's got her own, thanks. "I guess what I want to show is that it's O.K. to be athletic and feminine."

If nothing else, Katie Hnida gave us a rare moment, in which the homecoming queen walked off the field after the game and had little girls come up to her, saying, "Chin strap?" ❧

WHITE MEN CAN JUMP

DAN CRAY

The pose is classic Air Jordan. Legs spread wide and a basketball-laden arm arced high, a kid soars through the air of the Crenshaw High School gymnasium into the waiting arms of two grinning teammates, who heave him up toward the rim. The basketball slams haplessly off the forward edge to the roar of "Milk! Milk! Milk!" "You wait for Milk to dunk," quips teammate Jonathan Stokes, "you'll be waiting every game."

It's a stereotype, and the players know it, which is why they poke fun at it. "Milk" is David Meriwether, 17, 5 ft. 11 in., a junior whose mere presence at the Los Angeles school dropped more jaws than his first dunk ever could. When Meriwether stepped onto the court for Crenshaw's first regular-season game, he became the first white basketball player in the school's 30-year history. Meriwether's introduction at a recent preseason scrimmage prompted more than 1,000 students to stomp and chant his politically incorrect nickname. "I don't care what color the guys are, I just want to play," says the dazed Meriwether, "and there's no better school to play for."

To say Crenshaw High is steeped in basketball tradition is like saying the Boston Celtics have had some decent teams. The school's gym is littered with banners proclaiming

David Meriwether surrounded by his teammates

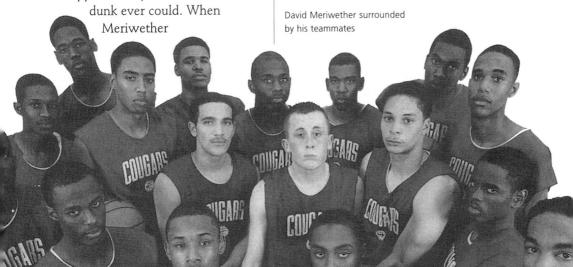

Crenshaw's 16 city titles and eight state championships. An astonishing 95% of the school's players have gone on to play college ball; eight have made it to the NBA.

But Crenshaw is an inner-city school, and doesn't let you forget it. Doorways are chained and gated; security guards outnumber grounds-keepers. Despite open enrollment, 81% of the 2,733 students are African American; most of the others are Hispanic. The school has only four white students, and Caucasian visitors are so rare that students automatically assume they're members of Meriwether's family.

No wonder then that no one expected Meriwether to actually enroll. "We've had white players who wanted to play here before," says Willie West, the team's coach for 29 years. "Then their mom visits the school, gets scared, and that's the end of it." But in an era in which good high school players switch teams like free agents, Meriwether was looking for a chance to play at a top school, regardless of the demographics.[1]

The decision initially produced a reversal of scenes played out years ago, when black players began breaking into white-dominated athletics. "The guys played me harder," Meriwether says. "Everybody called me 'white boy,' and I took a lot of elbows." But Meriwether, an easygoing kid who talks as if he's 30 and has an irrepressible sense of humor, played well enough to earn a spot on the team as backup point guard. "He's hard-nosed," says team-mate Richard Bluette, "and you've got to be because at this school they'll try to bring you down."

Meriwether shrugs it off but concedes, "Walking the halls can be a little uneasy. People say things, testing you." Classes have been routine, although Meriwether says one teacher discussed slavery by lecturing about "the white devil," prompting everyone in class to turn and stare at Meriwether. "I was like, Daaamn!" he says. "I can understand why people come out of here angry if that's how they're taught."

Teammates are satisfied that Meriwether is "just another player" and resent the notion that Crenshaw players would be anything but color blind. "Milk's no white Jackie Robinson," notes Eric Baker, "because we embraced Milk, and Jackie wasn't embraced by his teammates."

That was apparent during presea-son workouts, with Meriwether comfortable enough to razz fellow players. He now spends weekends hanging with teammates at "parties in the hood," while maintaining a B average. "Milk is like a chameleon," says Bluette. "He just blends in." If that's true, Meriwether's experiment at Crenshaw High will be all net. ∾

1 **demographics:** the characteristics of a population, such as age, income, education, and gender

JOAN BENOIT

1984 U.S. Olympic Marathon Gold Medalist

RINA FERRARELLI

During the third mile
not the eighteenth as expected
she surged ahead
leaving behind the press
of bodies, the breath
hot on her back
and set a pace
the expert claimed
she couldn't possibly keep
to the end.

Sure, determined,
moving to an inner rhythm
measuring herself against herself
alone in a field of fifty
she gained the twenty-six miles
of concrete, asphalt and humid weather
and burst into the roar of the crowd
to run the lap around the stadium
at the same pace
once to finish the race
and then again in victory

and she was still fresh
and not even out of breath
and standing.

WHEN THE BOYS
TAUGHT THEIR COACH

RICHARD ALAN NESBITT

Bryan was a solid fellow with fingers as soft as pillows. He looked over at me, brushed back a lock of auburn hair and tried to calm himself as he stood in the batter's box.

Three times he had missed the ball completely, striking only the black rubber tee on which I had placed the ball. I called out in encouragement: "Attaboy, Bryan! Keep your eye on the ball!"

I willed him to swing so his bat would connect solidly, the way I had coached him. As I watched this young man, so determined to do his best, my thoughts flashed back to another summer day in another park.

My sister Jennifer was playing on the swings when a little girl came up behind her to give her a friendly push. Jenny, who was only four or five at the time, took one look at the wide-open, almond-shaped eyes and flattened features and became hysterical, screaming and running toward the safety of her big brother, me. Jenny had been frightened by a Down syndrome child. A handicapped child like Bryan.

I calmed Jenny down, but I couldn't help noticing the pain in the disabled girl's eyes. She, too, began to cry, tears rolling down her face. With a lump in my throat, I watched her walk away.

Who knows why certain memories stick with you? That memory was burned into me for a lifetime. It helps explain why I got involved in the Special Olympics program in Los Angeles as an assistant coach.

Turning my attention back to Bryan, I heard the sound of a Louisville Slugger connecting with the hard rubber of a tee. For a moment it looked as if he might cry.

"Bryan, I think you're swinging a little too hard," I said, remaining upbeat. "Try taking it a bit easier. Just meet the ball." I reached around his shoulders and placed my hands over his on the bat, just as I had during so many other practice sessions. "Like this," I said, showing him once more the proper trajectory his swing should take.

As always, he took my advice and gave me a cheery smile.

This time he connected squarely. The softball blooped over the shortstop's head and rolled into the gap between left and center field. Grinning broadly, clapping his hands in glee, Bryan dropped the bat and ran toward first base amid the cheers of his teammates and coaches.

But now I groaned silently as I watched our defense try to field the ball. Bryan is one of the slowest runners on the team. Nevertheless, he managed a stand-up triple.

Our team was winless thus far in the season, and watching them lose game after game had left me feeling hollow. Just once I wanted them to feel the thrill of victory.

In a world where instant gratification teaches children to quit when the going gets tough, tough is what most of these kids' lives are all about. Some of the most basic acts—tying shoelaces or climbing stairs—are arduous tasks. Yet through it all, I've never known one of them to throw in the towel.

As a Marine Corps veteran, I've seen my share of tough times. From basic training on Parris Island in South Carolina to jungle survival training in the Philippines, we were taught never to give up no matter how insurmountable the odds. In these kids I've seen many of the same traits. Their determination and zest for accomplishment have taught me to push harder in my life.

This was our last practice before we departed for a four-day sports camp in San Luis Obispo, Calif., 200 miles up the coast. There we would get one final chance to redeem ourselves.

Several weeks later Paul Stanza, our head coach, and I took our team to San Luis Obispo. As we chauffeured them around to the various events, the boys and I enjoyed singing along with the radio. Rousing choruses were often heard pouring from our vehicles at stop signs.

On the final day of camp came our long-awaited softball tournament. Teams from all around the state were there, and everyone's spirits were high. During the van ride over to the ball field, a familiar song came over the radio: "Heroes" by David Bowie. We had just enough time to hear the song to completion before we reached our destination.

The van emptied. The players scrambled toward the field except for Bryan and his friend Blythe.

Blythe is an ardent Chicago Cubs fan. The only cap he would wear was a Cubs hat. He even slept with it on. Blythe looked up at me and said, "If Ernie were here watching us today, maybe we could be heroes." Ernie Banks, the most famous Chicago Cub ever, was Blythe's idol. I was actually a little surprised that he had made that connection between the song and the team.

"Yeah, couldn't we?" Bryan added eagerly.

Their eyes shone bright with hope. "Maybe so," I agreed.

The final match of the day pitted our team against one from San Diego. Both teams played hard, and as the game neared its end, I suddenly knew how every father must feel at his child's Little League game. I desperately wanted my kids to experience the win that had eluded them all season. I forgot all about sportsmanship.

I had my batters step out of the box right before the pitch in order to shake up the opposing pitcher. In Special Olympics play, the runner usually stops at whatever base his hit warrants. But I waved my runners on, knowing they had a better chance of making it to the next base than the opposition had of throwing them out.

It was a 3–3 tie in the final inning, and we had last ups. Bryan beat out a scratch base hit. Then Blythe smacked a line drive over second base, and Bryan came pounding around third. I felt myself choking up as Bryan crossed the plate.

Then both teams began to celebrate, and it was hard to tell the winning team from the losing side. They were cheering and hugging and applauding as though they all had just won the World Series itself.

As I looked on, humbled, I realized what these special kids had known all along. Nobody had lost. Everybody had gained, including me. The world isn't just about who wins, they showed me. Sometimes all that matters is that you go out and give it your all, constantly striving to better yourself. They had all made new friends, and they had all participated in the game. That was what really mattered.

As I stood in front of our dugout reflecting on this lesson, I felt somebody wrap his arms around me in a fierce bearhug. It was Bryan, beaming at me with pride and delight. I felt a warmth run through my entire body as I tightly hugged him back.

Then I remembered what Blythe had said to me earlier. You are heroes, I thought. Each and every one of you. ❧

Unsportsmanlike Conduct

Dave Barry

I first got involved in organized sports in fifth grade, when, because of federal law, I had to join the Little League. In Little League we played a game that is something like baseball, except in baseball you are supposed to catch, throw and hit a ball, whereas most of us Little Leaguers could do none of these things.

Oh, there were a few exceptions, fast-developing boys with huge quantities of adolescent hormones raging through their bodies, causing them to have rudimentary mustaches and giving them the ability to throw a ball at upwards of six hundred miles an hour, but with no idea whatsoever where it would go. These boys always got to pitch, which presented a real problem for the rest of us, because in Little League the pitcher stands eight feet from home plate. The catcher got to wear many protective garments, and the umpire got to wear protective garments *and* hide behind the catcher. But all we batters got to wear was plastic helmets that fell off if we moved our heads.

I hated to bat. I used to pray that the kids ahead of me would strike out, or that I would get appendicitis, or that a volcano would erupt in center field before my turn came. I was very close to God when I was in Little League. But sometimes He would let me down, and I'd have to bat. In the background, the coach would yell idiot advice, such as "Keep your eye on the ball." This was easy for *him* to say: he always stood over by the bench, well out of harm's way.

I made no effort to keep my eye on the ball. I concentrated exclusively on avoiding death. I would stand there, trying to hold my head perfectly still so my helmet wouldn't fall off, and when the prematurely large kid who was pitching let go of the ball, I would swing the bat violently, in hopes of striking out or deflecting the ball before it could smash into my body. Usually I struck out, which was good, because then I could go back to the safety of the bench and help the coach encourage some other terrified kid to keep his eye on the ball. I much preferred to play in the field, especially the outfield. If a batter got a hit, you could run like a maniac, and the odds were that you'd be several hundred feet away from the ball by the time it landed.

I understand that Little League was supposed to teach me the rules of sportsmanship. The main rule of sportsmanship I learned was: Never participate in a sport where the coach urges you to do insane and dangerous things that he himself does not do. Football is another good example. If you watch a football game, you'll notice that the coaches constantly urge the players to run into each other at high speeds, but the coaches themselves tend to remain on the sidelines.

So after I fulfilled my legal commitment to Little League, I avoided organized sports and got my exercise in the form of minor vandalism. But when I got to high school, I discovered that I had to go out for an organized sport so I could be called up to the auditorium stage during the annual athletic awards assembly to receive a varsity letter.

I cannot overemphasize the importance the kids in my high school attached to varsity letters. You could be a bozo of astonishing magnitude, but if you had a varsity letter, you were bound to succeed socially. Oh, the school administrators tried to make academic achievements seem important, too. They'd have academic assemblies, where they'd call all the studious kids up onto the stage. But the rest of the kids were unimpressed. They'd sit there, wearing their varsity sweaters, and hoot and snicker while some poor kid with a slide rule[1] dangling from his belt got the Math Achievement Award. No, to make it in my high school you had to have a varsity letter, which meant you had to go out for a sport.

So in my sophomore year I went out for track, because track was the sport where you were least likely to have something thrown at you or have somebody run into you at high speed. The event I chose was the long jump, because all you had to do was run maybe fifty feet, after which you leaped into a soft pit. That was it. The long jump was far superior to the other events, in which you were required to run as much as a mile without stopping.

---

1 **slide rule:** a ruler-like device used for making calculations

Anyway, I spent a happy spring, leaping into the pit and dreaming about going up on the stage to get my varsity letter. Then one day we all piled into buses and rode, laughing and gesturing at motorists, to a rival school for a track meet. This proved to be my downfall, because it turned out that at track meets they measured how far we long jumpers jumped, and only the three longest jumpers got points, which you needed to get your varsity letter. I was not one of the three longest jumpers. I was not one of the ten longest jumpers. In fact, they could have pulled people out of the crowd, old people with arthritis, and *they* probably would have jumped farther than I did.

So that was the end of my involvement with organized sports. Fortunately, there was one other avenue to popularity in my high school, which was to go to a dance, and behave in such an extremely antisocial manner that you got thrown out by the assistant principal in full view of hundreds of admiring kids. So in the end I achieved social acceptance.

After I got out of high school, varsity letters seemed less important, and academic achievement started to seem more important. I mean, if you go to a cocktail party and subtly contrive to flash your varsity letter, people will think you are a jerk; whereas if you subtly contrive to flash your Phi Beta Kappa[2] key, people will still think you are a jerk, but an educated jerk.

I often wonder what my former classmates do with their varsity letters, now that they're out of high school. Maybe they wear them in the privacy of their homes. ∿

---

2 **Phi Beta Kappa:** an honor society for college graduates who receive high grades

JUST ONCE

THOMAS J. DYGARD

Everybody liked the Moose. To his father and mother he was Bryan—as in Bryan Jefferson Crawford—but to everyone at Bedford City High he was the Moose. He was large and strong, as you might imagine from his nickname, and he was pretty fast on his feet—sort of nimble, you might say—considering his size. He didn't have a pretty face but he had a quick and easy smile—"sweet," some of the teachers called it; "nice," others said.

But on the football field, the Moose was neither sweet nor nice. He was just strong and fast and a little bit devastating as the left tackle of the Bedford City Bears. When the Moose blocked somebody, he stayed blocked. When the Moose was called on to open a hole in the line for one of the Bears' runners, the hole more often than not resembled an open garage door.

Now in his senior season, the Moose had twice been named to the all-conference team and was considered a cinch for all-state. He spent a lot of his spare time, when he wasn't in a classroom or on the football field, reading letters from colleges eager to have the Moose pursue higher education—and football—at their institution.

But the Moose had a hang-up.

He didn't go public with his hang-up until the sixth game of the season. But, looking back, most of his teammates agreed that probably the Moose had been nurturing the hang-up secretly for two years or more.

The Moose wanted to carry the ball.

For sure, the Moose was not the first interior lineman in the history of football, or even the history of Bedford City High, who banged heads up front and wore bruises like badges of honor—and dreamed of racing down the field with the ball to the end zone while everybody in the bleachers screamed his name.

But most linemen, it seems, are able to stifle the urge. The idea may pop into their minds from time to time, but in their hearts they know they can't run fast enough, they know they can't do that fancy dancing to elude tacklers, they know they aren't trained to read blocks. They know that their strengths and talents are best utilized in the line. Football is, after all, a team sport, and everyone plays the position where he most helps the team. And so these linemen, or most of them, go back to banging heads without saying the first word about the dream that flickered through their minds.

Not so with the Moose.

That sixth game, when the Moose's hang-up first came into public view, had ended with the Moose truly in all his glory as the Bears' left tackle. Yes, glory—but uncheered and sort of anonymous. The Bears were trailing 21–17 and had the ball on Mitchell High's five-yard line, fourth down, with time running out. The rule in such a situation is simple—the best back carries the ball behind the best blocker—and it is a rule seldom violated by those in control of their faculties. The Bears, of course, followed the rule. That meant Jerry Dixon running behind the Moose's blocking. With the snap of the ball, the Moose knocked down one lineman, bumped another one aside, and charged forward to flatten an approaching linebacker. Jerry did a little jig behind the Moose and then ran into the end zone, virtually untouched, to win the game.

After circling in the end zone a moment while the cheers echoed through the night, Jerry did run across and hug the Moose, that's true. Jerry knew who had made the touchdown possible.

But it wasn't the Moose's name that everybody was shouting. The fans in the bleachers were cheering Jerry Dixon.

It was probably at that precise moment that the Moose decided to go public.

In the dressing room, Coach Buford Williams was making his rounds among the cheering players and came to a halt in front of the Moose. "It was your great blocking that did it," he said.

"I want to carry the ball," the Moose said.

Coach Williams was already turning away and taking a step toward the next player due an accolade when his brain registered the fact that the

Moose had said something strange. He was expecting the Moose to say, "Aw, gee, thanks, Coach." That was what the Moose always said when the coach issued a compliment. But the Moose had said something else. The coach turned back to the Moose, a look of disbelief on his face. "What did you say?"

"I want to carry the ball."

Coach Williams was good at quick recoveries, as any high-school football coach had better be. He gave a tolerant smile and a little nod and said, "You keep right on blocking, son."

This time Coach Williams made good on his turn and moved away from the Moose.

The following week's practice and the next Friday's game passed without further incident. After all, the game was a road game over at Cartwright High, thirty-five miles away. The Moose wanted to carry the ball in front of the Bedford City fans.

Then the Moose went to work.

He caught up with the coach on the way to the practice field on Wednesday. "Remember," he said, leaning forward and down a little to get his face in the coach's face, "I said I want to carry the ball."

Coach Williams must have been thinking about something else because it took him a minute to look up into the Moose's face, and even then he didn't say anything.

"I meant it," the Moose said.

"Meant what?"

"I want to run the ball."

"Oh," Coach Williams said. Yes, he remembered. "Son, you're a great left tackle, a great blocker. Let's leave it that way."

The Moose let the remaining days of the practice week and then the game on Friday night against Edgewood High pass while he reviewed strategies. The review led him to Dan Blevins, the Bears' quarterback. If the signal-caller would join in, maybe Coach Williams would listen.

"Yeah, I heard," Dan said. "But, look, what about Joe Wright at guard, Bill Slocum at right tackle, even Herbie Watson at center. They might all want to carry the ball. What are we going to do—take turns? It doesn't work that way."

So much for Dan Blevins.

The Moose found that most of the players in the backfield agreed with Dan. They couldn't see any reason why the Moose should carry the ball, especially in place of themselves. Even Jerry Dixon, who owed a lot of his glory to the Moose's blocking, gaped in disbelief at the Moose's idea. The Moose, however, got some support from his fellow linemen. Maybe they had dreams of their own, and saw value in a precedent.[1]

As the days went by, the word spread—not just on the practice field and in the corridors of Bedford City High, but all around town. The players by now were openly taking sides. Some thought it a jolly good idea that the Moose carry the ball. Others, like Dan Blevins, held to the purist line—a left tackle plays left tackle, a ballcarrier carries the ball, and that's it.

Around town, the vote wasn't even close. Everyone wanted the Moose to carry the ball.

"Look, son," Coach Williams said to the Moose on the practice field the Thursday before the Benton Heights game, "this has gone far enough. Fun is fun. A joke is a joke. But let's drop it."

"Just once," the Moose pleaded.

Coach Williams looked at the Moose and didn't answer.

The Moose didn't know what that meant.

The Benton Heights Tigers were duck soup for the Bears, as everyone knew they would be. The Bears scored in their first three possessions and led 28–0 at the half. The hapless Tigers had yet to cross the fifty-yard line under their own steam.

All the Bears, of course, were enjoying the way the game was going, as were the Bedford City fans jamming the bleachers.

Coach Williams looked irritated when the crowd on a couple of occasions broke into a chant: "Give the Moose the ball! Give the Moose the ball!"

On the field, the Moose did not know whether to grin at hearing his name shouted by the crowd or to frown because the sound of his name was irritating the coach. Was the crowd going to talk Coach Williams into putting the Moose in the backfield? Probably not; Coach Williams didn't bow to that kind of pressure. Was the coach going to refuse to give the ball to the Moose just to show the crowd—and the Moose and the rest of the players—who was boss? The Moose feared so.

In his time on the sideline, when the defensive unit was on the field, the Moose, of course, said nothing to Coach Williams. He knew better than to break the coach's concentration during a game—even a runaway

---

1 **precedent:** an incident that might serve as an example to justify a similar action later

victory—with a comment on any subject at all, much less his desire to carry the ball. As a matter of fact, the Moose was careful to stay out of the coach's line of vision, especially when the crowd was chanting "Give the Moose the ball!"

By the end of the third quarter the Bears were leading 42–0.

Coach Williams had been feeding substitutes into the game since half-time, but the Bears kept marching on. And now, in the opening minutes of the fourth quarter, the Moose and his teammates were standing on the Tigers' five-yard line, about to pile on another touchdown.

The Moose saw his substitute, Larry Hinden, getting a slap on the behind and then running onto the field. The Moose turned to leave.

Then he heard Larry tell the referee, "Hinden for Holbrook."

Holbrook? Chad Holbrook, the fullback?

Chad gave the coach a funny look and jogged off the field.

Larry joined the huddle and said, "Coach says the Moose at fullback and give him the ball."

Dan Blevins said, "Really?"

"Really."

The Moose was giving his grin—"sweet," some of the teachers called it; "nice," others said.

"I want to do an end run," the Moose said.

Dan looked at the sky a moment, then said, "What does it matter?"

The quarterback took the snap from center, moved back and to his right while turning, and extended the ball to the Moose.

The Moose took the ball and cradled it in his right hand. So far, so good. He hadn't fumbled. Probably both Coach Williams and Dan were surprised.

He ran a couple of steps and looked out in front and said aloud, "Whoa!"

Where had all those tacklers come from?

The whole world seemed to be peopled with players in red jerseys—the red of the Benton Heights Tigers. They all were looking straight at the Moose and advancing toward him. They looked very determined, and not friendly at all. And there were so many of them. The Moose had faced tough guys in the line, but usually one at a time, or maybe two. But this—five or six. And all of them heading for him.

The Moose screeched to a halt, whirled, and ran the other way.

Dan Blevins blocked somebody in a red jersey breaking through the middle of the line, and the Moose wanted to stop running and thank him.

But he kept going.

His reverse had caught the Tigers' defenders going the wrong way, and the field in front of the Moose looked open. But his blockers were going the wrong way, too. Maybe that was why the field looked so open. What did it matter, though, with the field clear in front of him? This was going to be a cakewalk; the Moose was going to score a touchdown.

Then, again—"Whoa!"

Players with red jerseys were beginning to fill the empty space—a lot of them. And they were all running toward the Moose. They were kind of low, with their arms spread, as if they wanted to hit him hard and then grab him.

A picture of Jerry Dixon dancing his little jig and wriggling between tacklers flashed through the Moose's mind. How did Jerry do that? Well, no time to ponder that one right now.

The Moose lowered his shoulder and thundered ahead, into the cloud of red jerseys. Something hit his left thigh. It hurt. Then something pounded his hip, then his shoulder. They both hurt. Somebody was hanging on to him and was a terrible drag. How could he run with somebody hanging on to him? He knew he was going down, but maybe he was across the goal. He hit the ground hard, with somebody coming down on top of him, right on the small of his back.

The Moose couldn't move. They had him pinned. Wasn't the referee supposed to get these guys off?

Finally the load was gone and the Moose, still holding the ball, got to his knees and one hand, then stood.

He heard the screaming of the crowd, and he saw the scoreboard blinking.

He had scored.

His teammates were slapping him on the shoulder pads and laughing and shouting.

The Moose grinned, but he had a strange and distant look in his eyes.

He jogged to the sideline, the roars of the crowd still ringing in his ears.

"Okay, son?" Coach Williams asked.

The Moose was puffing. He took a couple of deep breaths. He relived for a moment the first sight of a half dozen players in red jerseys, all with one target—him. He saw again the menacing horde of red jerseys that had risen up just when he'd thought he had clear sailing to the goal. They all zeroed in on him, the Moose, alone.

The Moose glanced at the coach, took another deep breath, and said, "Never again." ∾

Responding to Cluster Two

What Does It Mean to Be an Athlete?
Thinking Skill ANALYZING

1. Do you think girls should be able to play on boys' teams? Why or why not?

2. What if Rich Nesbitt in "When the Boys Taught the Coach" was called out of town? **Analyze** which character in cluster one or two would be the best substitute coach. Explain your answer.

3. **Hyperbole** is extreme exaggeration used for emphasis. **Analyze**, or find examples in, "Unsportsmanlike Conduct" that show how Dave Barry uses hyperbole to create humor.

4. In a team sport each athlete has a defined role and is expected to perform that role for the good of the team. Do you think The Moose in "Just Once" is selfish and hurts the team when he asks to carry the ball?

5. **Analyze** the main characters in this cluster by listing three of their strongest qualities, attitudes, or abilities. Use your analysis to decide which character or person you would want with you on a team. Be prepared to explain your cloice.

Name	Qualities
Katie Hnida	
David Meriwether	
Joan Benoit	
boys on the baseball team	
Dave Barry	
the Moose	

Writing Activity: The Most Valuable Player

Use the selections and charts from clusters one and two and **analyze** whom you would choose for a "most valuable player" award. Write a nomination speech to **persuade** your classmates to accept your candidate.

Strong Persuasive Writing

- begins with a statement of the writer's opinion

- uses facts, quotes, examples, and so forth to support the opinion

- is organized for maximum impact, often with the most persuasive arguments presented last

- presents information clearly and logically

- concludes by restating the writer's opinion

CLUSTER THREE

Is Winning Everything?

Thinking Skill   INFERRING

Dying to Win

Merrell Noden

Christy Henrich's fiancé, Bo Moreno, loved her for her sweet side, but he also knew her demons. That's why, when Henrich's parents were preparing to check her into the Menninger Clinic in Topeka, Kansas, for treatment of her eating disorders, Moreno warned them to inspect her suitcase carefully. "It had a false bottom," he says. "She had lined the entire bottom of the suitcase with laxatives. That was part of her addiction." Henrich weighed 63 pounds at the time.

At another treatment center about a year later, the staff had to confine her to a wheelchair to prevent her from running everywhere in an attempt to lose weight. "Another part of the addiction," says Moreno. "Constant movement. Anything to burn calories."

At the peak of her career as a world-class gymnast, the 4'10" Henrich weighed 95 pounds. But when she died on July 26, eight days past her 22nd birthday, of multiple organ failure at Research Medical Center in Kansas City, she was down to 61 pounds. And that actually represented improvement. On July 4, the day she was discharged from St. Joseph's (Missouri) Medical Center, she had weighed 47 pounds.

"She was getting intensive supportive care," says Dr. David McKinsey, who treated Henrich during the last week of her life, the final three days of which were spent in a coma. "But a person passes the point of no return, and then, no matter how aggressive the care is, it doesn't work. The major problem is a severe lack of fuel. The person becomes so malnourished that the liver doesn't work, the kidneys don't work, and neither do the muscles. The cells no longer function."

Christy Henrich at Olympic trials
in Austin, Texas, 1988

Henrich had been in and out of so many hospitals over the past two years that Moreno lost count of them. Her medical bills ran to more than $100,000. There were occasional periods of hope, when she would gain weight and seem to be making progress. But for the most part, as Henrich herself told Dale Brendel of The Independence [Missouri] Examiner, "my life is a horrifying nightmare. It feels like there's a beast inside me, like a monster. It feels evil."

Henrich's funeral was held at St. Mary's Catholic Church in Independence. Her pink casket sat at the front of the church as several hundred mourners filed in. Some were fellow gymnasts; some were friends and relatives; some were former classmates at Fort Osage High, where Henrich had been a straight-A student. In his eulogy Moreno asked those present to do what most people had always had trouble doing when Henrich was alive: to think of her as more than just a gymnast. "She was a talented artist and an unbelievable cook," he said. "But I must admit, her favorite hobby was shopping, for herself and others. . . . ."

Eating disorders are easily the gravest health problem facing female athletes, and they affect not just gymnasts but also swimmers, distance runners, tennis and volleyball players, divers and figure skaters. According to the American College of Sports Medicine, as many as 62% of females competing in "appearance" sports (like figure skating and gymnastics) and endurance sports suffer from an eating disorder. Julie Anthony, a touring tennis pro in the 1970s who now runs a sports-fitness clinic in Aspen, Colorado, has estimated that 30% of the women on the tennis tour suffer from some type of eating affliction. Peter Farrell, who has been coaching women's track and cross-country at Princeton for 17 years, puts the number of women runners with eating disorders even higher. "My experience is that 70% of my runners have dabbled in it in its many hideous forms."

Eating disorders, however, are by no means limited to athletes. The Association of Anorexia Nervosa and Associated Disorders reported before a U.S. Senate subcommittee hearing that 18% of females in the U.S. suffer from eating disorders. The illnesses tend to strike women who, like Henrich, are perfectionists, and they often seize those who seem to be the most successful. In 1983 singer Karen Carpenter died following a long battle with eating disorders, and for years Princess Diana waged a well-publicized fight against bulimia.

Girls or women who suffer from depression or low self-esteem are particularly susceptible to eating disorders, as are victims of sexual abuse. The expectations of society, particularly those regarding beauty, also play a role. Not coincidentally, the ideal of the perfect female body has changed dramatically in the past several decades. Marilyn Monroe, as she sashayed[1] away from Jack Lemmon and Tony Curtis in *Some Like It Hot*, looked like "Jell-O on springs." Lemmon's description was a compliment in 1959. A decade later it would make most women cringe.

Given the importance that sport attaches to weight—and, in the subjectively judged sports, to appearance—it isn't surprising that eating disorders are common among athletes. Nor is it surprising that they exact a far greater toll among women than men. In a 1992 NCAA[2] survey of collegiate athletics, 93% of the programs reporting eating disorders were in women's sports. It is true that some male athletes—wrestlers, for example—use extreme methods of weight loss, but there is an important difference between these and the self-starvation practiced by anorexics. A wrestler's perception of his body is not distorted. When he is not competing, he can return to a healthy weight. That is not the case with anorexics, trapped as they are behind bars they can't see.

A study conducted a few years ago at Penn found that while both men and women tend to be unrealistic about how others perceive their bodies, men's perceptions tend to be distorted positively, while women's are more likely to be negative. . . . .

"Men grow into what they're supposed to be," says Mary T. Meagher, the world-record holder in the 100- and 200-meter butterfly events. "They're supposed to be big and muscular. A woman's body naturally produces more fat. We grow away from what we're supposed to be as athletes."

Though laymen tend to lump anorexia and bulimia together—perhaps because experimentation with bulimia often leads to anorexia—the two are markedly different. "In a way bulimia is more dangerous," says Pan Fanaritis, who has coached women's track at Georgetown, Missouri and Villanova and is now the men's and women's coach at Denison. "Anorexia you can see."

---

1 **sashayed:** strutted

2 **NCAA:** National Collegiate Athletic Association, the rulemaking body of college athletics

What you see is frightening. Anorexia is self-starvation driven by a distorted perception of one's appearance. It is not unusual for an anorexic who is 5' 8" to weigh 100 pounds or less—and still think she's too fat. . . . .

The long-term consequences of anorexia are catastrophic. Deprived of calcium, the body steals it from the bones, leading to osteoporosis. "I've seen X-rays where the bones look like honeycomb," says Fanaritis. "X-rays of an anorexic of four or five years and those of a 70-year-old are very similar." Anorexics have suffered stress fractures just walking down the street.

Bulimia is a binge-purge syndrome in which huge quantities of food—sometimes totaling as much as 20,000 calories in a day—are consumed in a short period of time and then expelled through self-induced vomiting, excessive exercise, the use of diuretics[3] or laxatives, or some combination of those methods. Stomach acids rot the teeth of bulimics and, if they are sticking their fingers down their throats to induce vomiting, their fingernails. Their throats get swollen and lacerated.[4] Electrolyte imbalances[5] disrupt their heart rates. But since bulimics are usually of normal weight, years may pass before a parent, roommate or spouse learns the terrible secret.

"You can always find an empty bathroom," says one recovering bulimic who was an All-America distance runner at Texas. During her worst period of self-abuse she was visiting bathrooms five or six times a day, vomiting simply by flexing her stomach muscles. "It's like a drug," she says of the syndrome. "It controls you. An overwhelming feeling comes over you, like a fog."

In the 1992 NCAA survey 51% of the women's gymnastics programs that responded reported eating disorders among team members, a far greater percentage than in any other sport. The true number is almost certainly higher. Moreno says he knows of five gymnasts on the national team who have eating disorders. Bob Ito, the former women's gymnastics coach at Washington, has estimated that on some of his teams 40% of the athletes had "outright eating disorders." One world-class gymnast has admitted that while she was at UCLA the entire team

---

3 **diuretics:** medicine that increases the need to go to the bathroom

4 **lacerated:** cut

5 **Electrolyte imbalances:** a lack of sodium, potassium, and chloride needed to help the body retain fluids

would binge and vomit together following meets. It was, she said, a "social thing."

Anorexia offers a convenient antidote to what young gymnasts dread most—the onset of womanhood. Not only do anorexics keep their boyish figures, but many go months or even years without their menstrual periods, a side effect that contributes to osteoporosis. "This is a matter of locked-on adolescence," says Scott Pengelly, a psychologist from Eugene, Oregon, who has treated athletes with eating disorders.

No one knows that better than Cathy Rigby, who 20 years ago was the darling of U.S. gymnastics and paid for it with 12 years of bulimia. "As much as [the news of Henrich's death] makes me sad, it makes me angry," Rigby says. "This sort of thing has been going on for so long in our sport, and there's so much denial."

When Rigby competed, every story celebrated her girlishness, which she worked so hard to maintain that she pinned her pigtails back from her face, fastening them so tightly that she got headaches. And the image of the world-class gymnast as waif[6] has only become more exaggerated in the two decades since. The average size of the women on the U.S. Olympic gymnastics team has shrunk from 5'3", 105 pounds in 1976 to 4'9", 88 pounds in 1992. At the 1993 world championships the all-around gold medalist, 16-year-old Shannon Miller, was 4'10", 79 pounds.

What chance would Vera Caslavska have had in such company? Caslavska, who won the all-around titles at the 1964 and '68 Olympics, was a geriatric[7] giant by today's standards. In Mexico City the 26-year-old Czech was 5'3", 121 pounds. What's more, she and Ludmila Turischeva of the Soviet Union, who succeeded Caslavska as all-around champion, looked like women. Gold medal or not, Turischeva was upstaged in '68 by 13-year-old Olga Korbut, who was 4'11" and 85 pounds. Gymnastics has not been the same since.

At its highest levels gymnastics has evolved in a direction that is incompatible with a woman's mature body. That was plain when Nadia Comaneci, the darling of the 1976 Olympics, showed up at the world championships two years later having grown four inches and put on 21 pounds. She had become a woman, and as John Goodbody wrote in *The Illustrated History of Gymnastics*, "We learnt that week how perfection in women's gymnastics can be blemished by maturity."

---

6 **waif:** small, homeless child
7 **geriatric:** old; elderly

▲ ▲ ▲

Henrich's career followed a pattern not unlike that of thousands of little girls who fall in love with gymnastics the first time they see it on television. Henrich started at the age of four. When she was eight she enrolled at the Great American Gymnastics Express in the neighboring suburb of Blue Springs [Missouri]. Al Fong, a 41-year-old former LSU[8] gymnast, founded Great American in 1979, one year before Henrich joined. Even in a sport dominated by monomaniacal[9] men, Fong's determination to produce champion gymnasts is extraordinary. "I work at this seven days a week," he told a reporter last year, "and I look forward to doing it for the next 25 years. It's an obsession with me."

Fong's elite gymnasts are renowned for the hours they train: one three-hour session at six in the morning and then four more hours at five in the afternoon. On meet days they are in the gym to work out two hours before the meet begins. "He pushed them really hard," says Sandy Henrich, Christy's mother. "He wanted them to train no matter what. He didn't want them to get casts [for fractures] because it took away their muscle tone."

For intensity Fong met his match in Henrich. Her nickname at the club was E.T.—Extra-Tough—and she more than lived up to it, competing with stress fractures and placing second all around in the U.S. nationals just three months after she broke her neck in 1989. "No one can force someone to train 32 hours a week unless they really want to," Fong said last week. "The sacrifices are too great. Christy worked five times harder than anybody else. She became so good because she worked so hard and had this kind of focus."

Henrich made sensational progress. In 1986, at age 14, she finished fifth at the national junior championships and competed in her first international meet, in Italy. In early 1988, when she finished 10th in the all-around competition at the senior nationals, her dream of making the U.S. team at that year's Olympics seemed attainable.

"What's a [high school] dance compared to the Olympics?" she said when she was 15. "It's what I want to do. I want it so bad. I know I have a chance for the Olympics, and that gets me fired up." But

8 **LSU:** Louisiana State University

9 **monomaniacal:** excessive concentration on one thought or idea

Henrich didn't make the Olympic team in 1988. She missed a berth[10] by 0.118 of a point in a vault in the compulsories.[11]

▲ ▲ ▲

In 1989 Henrich had her best year as a gymnast. She finished second in the all-around at the U.S. championships and fourth in the world championships in the uneven parallel bars. By that time she also had a serious eating disorder.

Its inception can be traced in part to an incident in March 1988, at a meet in Budapest, when a U.S. judge remarked that Henrich would have to lose weight if she wanted to make the Olympic team. Sandy Henrich recalls meeting her daughter at the airport upon her return: "The minute she got off the plane, the first words out of her mouth were that she had to lose weight. A judge had told her she was fat. Christy was absolutely devastated. She had a look of panic on her face. And I had a look of panic on my face. She weighed 90 pounds and was beautiful."

Henrich began eating less and less, an apple a day at first, and then just a slice of apple—this while continuing to work out six, seven hours each day.

In one important respect Henrich was different from many anorexics, who tend to live solitary existences. During her junior year at Fort Osage High she began to date Moreno, a friend of her older brother, Paul, and a wrestler on the Fort Osage team. "She was always very tough on herself," says Moreno, "and I could relate to that." Indeed, he recalls that Henrich got jealous when she learned that his body fat was 8%, while hers was 9%. "I had to tell her men just have lower body fat," he says. They got engaged in 1990 and were to be married later that year, but the wedding had to be postponed when Henrich fell ill. "She wanted to live in Florida and become a nurse," says Moreno.

Soon after they began dating, Henrich asked Moreno how wrestlers lost weight. "I told her we'd wear plastic. Run in the shower with the steam on. Take Ex-Lax. And," he recalls with a wince, "every one of the things I told her, she tried. That laid real guilt on me, but I had no idea she'd do it. I had always told her how stupid it was."

---

10 **berth:** place

11 **compulsories:** in gymnastics, the round where certain techniques must be performed exactly

Moreno says Fong might have spotted the danger signals of anorexia and bulimia earlier. "I find it hard to believe Al would not notice that every day Christy would work out, run five miles and come back. She truly loved Al and would have done anything for him. He'd say, 'Tuck your stomach in. You look like the Pillsbury Doughboy.' "

Fong denies ever harping on Henrich's weight or making the Doughboy comment. "It's just not true," he says. "I've heard those comments. Where in the world does that come from?"

Moreno and Sandy and Paul Henrich agree that the blame for Christy's obsession with weight should not fall only on her coach. "It's the whole system," says Sandy. "No matter what you do, it's never, never enough. The whole system has got to change—parents, coaches, the federation."

Christy lived at home, and a former USA Gymnastics official suggests that her parents might have pushed harder for intervention. As Christy's weight dropped precipitously,[12] "they had to be aware of it," the official says, adding that the federation received no complaints from the family. Some of Henrich's friends question if they, too, should have seen the signs earlier.

Moreno has come to understand Henrich's compulsion. "Christy's also to blame for her perfectionist attitude," he says. "The disease strikes people like that. I can remember Christy telling me, 'There's only one first place. Second place sucks.' "

Gail Vaughn, the director of Reforming Feelings, a counseling service in Liberty, Missouri, worked with Henrich for six months. "Probably one of the things that worked against her most was that label, E.T.," says Vaughn. "She learned to deny pain. She competed in one of her biggest meets with a stress fracture. So when her body broke down and screamed in pain, she ignored it. Because she had learned to push past the pain."

▲ ▲ ▲

For women, eating disorders are "like steroids are for men," says Liz Natale, a recovering anorexic who was a member of the Texas team that won the 1986 NCAA cross-country title. "You'll get results, but you'll pay for it."

For a time you do get results. That's part of the seduction. As an athlete's weight falls, his or her aerobic power increases. And psychologi-

12 **precipitously:** dropping steeply

cally there is no lash like anorexia. "To be a great competitor, you need that tunnel vision that anorexia feeds on," says Farrell. "Anybody who can starve herself can run a 10,000 really well."

But ultimately eating disorders exact a severe psychological toll. Distance runner Mary Wazeter was so tormented by constant thoughts of food that in February 1982, after withdrawing from Georgetown in her freshman year, she jumped from a bridge into the ice-covered Susquehanna River in her hometown of Wilkes-Barre, Pennslyvania. Her suicide attempt failed, but she broke her back and will spend the rest of her life in a wheelchair. . . .

Regrettably, too many coaches see only what they want to see. Says Fanaritis, a college track coach: "How about the football coach who has the kid come back from summer vacation and he's gained 60 pounds and his neck has grown two inches, and the kid says, 'I lifted my a.. off'? It's the same issue. You're not the one who said, 'Go home and use steroids.' You're not the one who said, 'Get skinny so you can run fast.' But you're in that middle ground."

Spurred by Henrich's case, USA Gymnastics has begun to take measures seeking to help prevent eating disorders. Last year the federation measured the bone density of all 32 national team members and found that three of them had deficiencies. It says it is trying to teach young gymnasts that they can say no if they feel too much is being asked by a coach. But how realistic is it to expect children to stop themselves from doing something they love? Especially when, as famed women's gymnastics coach Bela Karolyi once put it, "The young ones are the greatest little suckers in the world. They will follow you no matter what."

▲　▲　▲

Christy Henrich was buried at St. Mary's Cemetery in Independence [Missouri]. A line of cars half a mile long moved slowly through the tombstones, which marked the graves of those who had lived 70, 80, even 90 years. For Henrich the time was tragically short. The inscription on her stone reads: 1972–1994. ∾

GRANNY ED AND
THE LEWISVILLE RAIDERS

RAE RAINEY

It never occurred to me that Granny Ed was different from other grandmothers. Her name was out of the ordinary, but she always said, "If your parents put a handle like Edwinalou on you, you'd prefer a nickname too." It made good sense to me. She had normal grandmother interests like knitting, baking, and attending my basketball games.

Basketball! I eat and sleep the sport, but right then I wished I'd never heard of it. Our high school team had basketball Trouble, and I mean Trouble with a capital T.

Coach Marshall was a super coach, and we had high hopes of finishing first in the district this year. What happened? December second, Coach Marshall had a car accident over by Murphy Junction. He ended up in the hospital with a broken back and will be in the hospital two months—plus a long convalescence. To make matters worse, the only other man teacher in our high school is Mr. LaFrance, who doesn't know whether you bounce, kick, or bury a basketball. That leaves the Lewisville Raiders coachless.

The team had gathered at our house, as usual, due to Granny Ed's weakness for feeding hungry ballplayers.

"Men, we've got troubles if the principal can't come up with someone to take Coach Marshall's place," Al James said, between huge bites of pizza.

SOMEBODY'S GRANDMOTHER
1983
Larry Zingale

"Wish my dad could help out, but he's working swing shift at the sawmill," said Leftie.

"If Grandpa Thor were still living, he would take over," I added sadly. "He was a great college coach before he died." The team nodded in sympathetic agreement and respect.

"If we could just get someone to come to the gym and supervise our practices, maybe we could stumble along until a replacement for Coach Marshall is found," Al said.

"That's easier said than done. All the teachers are already doubling up on classes," I said, feeling more discouraged every minute.

"Well, gentlemen, if a body is all you need at practice, I can certainly provide that," Granny Ed spoke from the doorway. "You're sure not going to let a little problem like this throw a monkey wrench in the Lewisville Raider team, are you?"

There was a long silence. I wanted to sink through the floor. Granny Ed at practice! Oh no! You've really done it this time, Granny Ed, I thought.

Al, who has a reputation for having a pretty cool head, was the first to speak. "You know, Granny Ed, I think if the principal OK's your offer, it would really help us out of a tough spot. We need help right now!"

The rest of the team nodded in approval.

That's how it all started. Granny Ed arrived promptly at three-thirty the next afternoon. Her knitting bag was under one arm, a newspaper under the other, and she was sporting the brightest pair of red tennis shoes I'd ever laid eyes on.

"Go right ahead with your practice, gentlemen. I'll just sit here and watch," she said, whipping out her spare knitting needle that was always secured in the thick braids on top of her head.

"OK, men, let's work on some man-to-man defense," Al yelled. "We've been pretty sloppy."

Buzzie and Leftie brought the ball down court. Mark Elingson was guarding Leftie, but with one quick move Leftie faked out Mark and went in for an easy shot.

"Run the play again," Al called out, "and this time, stay with your man, Mark."

Buzzie tossed the ball to Leftie. A quick move to his left and Leftie had another easy shot.

"What do you do with a left-handed shooter, Mark?" a voice shouted from the sidelines. Granny Ed leaped to her feet and was out on the floor, showing Mark exactly what he was doing wrong.

"You're positioning your body wrong for a left-handed shooter," she said. "And you, Al, you've been standing in the key at least ten seconds. Move in and out of there. In a game the referee would give the ball out-of-bounds to the other team," she scolded.

Al's face turned tomato-red, but he nodded in agreement. "Guess you're right, Granny Ed, but how do you know about basketball rules?"

"Gentlemen, I didn't sit for twenty-five years keeping statistics and watching Big Thor coach for nothing. There is very little I don't know about basketball."

From then on, it was Granny Ed all the way. She worked us so hard and long our tongues were hanging out, but we all knew it was the best practice session we'd had all season.

"See you tomorrow, Granny Ed," the team yelled as we headed out the gym doors for home.

"Goodbye, gentlemen." Granny Ed waved back happily.

She hummed to herself as we headed toward home. Suddenly she stopped. "I didn't embarrass you, did I, Sprout?" she asked anxiously. "Did I come on a little too strong at practice?" She studied my face carefully.

"No, Granny, you did just fine," I said, trying to sound convincing. "You really helped us out." What could it hurt? It would only be for a few days.

They say bad luck runs in streaks, but for our Lewisville Raiders it ran as wide as the Colorado River. At the end of the week, there was no new basketball coach.

"It is a financial impossibility for our small district to pay the salary of another teacher-coach, boys. Until the school board finds a volunteer to take over, you will simply have to make do," Mr. Fisch told us. "It is something over which I have no control," he said, shuffling the papers on his desk nervously.

That day, after practice, we gathered in the gym to discuss our problem.

"Granny Ed, what are we going to do?" Al asked.

"Tomorrow night, gentlemen, you have your first league game against Darby. They're the defending champions in the league, but I believe you have the ability to beat them. You've worked long and hard in practice, and you're ready for any team. If you're willing to put up with an old lady for one game, I'll do my very best to help. What do you say, gentlemen?"

The startled players looked from one to another. I stared a hole through the gym floor. I just couldn't bear to watch what was going to happen. Whispers passed from player to player, and then Al stood up.

"Granny Ed, we figure you've helped us in a tough situation. If you really mean it, we would be glad to have you coach the Raiders tomorrow night."

Granny Ed's face broke into a smile bright enough to light up all the western states. "Gentlemen," she said, in a choked voice, "you're going to be the winner."

Darby was three times the size of Lewisville, and their big gym was packed to the rafters as we made our entrance. Last one in the door was Granny Ed, her knitting bag under one arm and chalkboard under the other. She sat down primly on the Lewisville bench, placed her knitting bag beside her, the chalkboard on the floor, and folding her hands in her lap, watched intently every move we were making in warm-ups.

"I'm sorry, madam," the Darby coach said, moving toward Granny Ed. "This bench is reserved for the Lewisville Raiders and their coach. You'll have to move up in the stands with the other spectators."

"Young man, I am perfectly fine right here," Granny Ed said, gently pushing the Darby coach aside to watch our warm-ups.

"Don't you understand what I'm saying? Only the coach can sit here," he repeated loudly.

"Don't shout, young man. I heard you the first time. For your information, I am the coach," Granny Ed said, standing as tall as her five feet would stretch.

"You're what?" the Darby coach gasped. "You said you're what?" he repeated as though his hearing had failed.

"You heard me correctly. Now, if you will kindly move out of my way, I should like very much to watch my team's warm-up."

"This is absolutely unbelievable! I can't put my players out on the floor to play a little old lady's team."

"Well, I shall assume that if your team doesn't show up on the floor when the game whistle blows, you will forfeit the game to the Lewisville Raiders," Granny offered sweetly.

"Forfeit!" the Darby coach shouted. "We'll forfeit nothing. Just remember, Coach Whateveryournameis, you'll be treated the same as any other coach, even if you are a woman." He stamped back and plopped himself down on the far end of the Darby bench.

"Hothead, isn't he?" Granny Ed said with a twinkle in her eye. I knew right then Granny Ed had psyched out our first opponent.

Our fast break was super that night, and using a two-platoon system,

Granny Ed directed a complete rout of the Darby Bulldogs. When the game ended, the scoreboard read: Lewisville–85; Darby–55. It was the upset of the year, and one the people in Lewisville are still talking about.

At the end of the game, Granny Ed gathered up her knitting bag and her chalkboard. She walked quickly to the Darby coach for the traditional handshake and commented ever so sweetly, "The name is not Whateveryournameis, young man. The name is Granny Ed, coach of the Lewisville Raiders."

The Darby coach flinched, turned, and fled to the Darby dressing room. It was the Darby win that launched Granny Ed in her coaching career.

Our Lewisville Raiders, with Granny Ed as head coach, breezed through the fourteen-game league schedule undefeated; and we qualified for the state tournament. Granny Ed had become a celebrity throughout the state. Our phone rang with interview requests and well-wishers. Granny Ed seemed to thrive on all the excitement and was happier than I'd ever seen her.

The state tournament was serious business to Granny Ed, and our practices were no-nonsense and hard work. Next week, our team would travel to the city for our town's first appearance in a state tournament. Then we would find out if the Lewisville Raiders were really good or only a much-publicized curiosity.

The night before we left for the tournament, Granny Ed came into my room and sank down on the bed. Her usual smiling face was drawn and lined. "Sprout, I'm afraid this time I've overstepped my bounds. It was all right to coach against schools in our league, but next week we'll be competing against the big boys. I'm not sure I'm up to it. Maybe it's time for me to step aside."

I folded and refolded the shirt I was packing before I dared look up at her. "Granny Ed, you've taken us this far. Don't you think you owe it to the team to stay with us when the going gets rough?"

"It isn't that I don't want to. I just hope I don't let the team down." Managing a weak smile, she stood up and headed for the door. "Well, with the team behind me, and you behind me, and my picture splashed over half the newspapers in the state, there's just no telling what will happen. Right, Sprout?"

I gave her a big wink. "Granny Ed, nobody ever would have guessed we'd get this far. We'll give it all we've got and every one we win is for you."

▲ ▲ ▲

"King City, here we come!" Leftie shouted as the chartered bus, decorated from front to back with gaudy red and gold banners, entered the city limits. There was no turning back now. For better or for worse, our team was about to play in its first state tourney. Heaven help us and Granny Ed! I thought. And Grandpa Thor, if you have any pull up there, don't let the other teams pour it on too bad.

Each team in the tournament was given a practice session in the Coliseum before it competed in its first game. The Coliseum was unbelievably big. It seated 10,000, which was about 9,500 more than the Lewisville gym. Granny Ed could tell how nervous we all were.

"Gentlemen," she said, motioning for us to join her at the side of the gym floor. "You will notice that the playing floor is exactly the same size as our floor. The basket is precisely the same height from the floor. And according to my calculations, it should take no more energy to run up and down this floor, and put the ball through the hoop, than it does in our gym. Am I right?"

A resounding "Right!" was her answer.

With a twinkle in her eyes, Granny Ed went on, "Then I can assume, gentlemen, the player who is not able to do this effectively isn't putting out his all, and I shall personally jab that player with my knitting needle where it will do the most good. Right?"

That broke the team up and they shouted an even louder "Right!"

She had psyched the team out of a bad case of jitters. The only thing was . . . how long would it be before our magic bubble burst?

No one was more surprised or happy than Granny Ed and the Raider team when we swept with ease through the first three games on the winning side. By now, the Lewisville Raiders had become the Cinderella team of the tournament, the country bumpkins showing the city boys the finer points of the game. Headlines in the papers praised our team and Granny Ed.

GRANNY ED AND HER RIPPIN' RAIDERS WIN AGAIN met our eyes as we passed the newspaper stand. We headed for the last and final game—our chance for the state championship.

I don't know who kept the town going, or if they closed up completely, because I saw most of the people of Lewisville packed in the stands. The town's oldest resident, Emil Gunder, was waving a sign saying: GIVE IT TO 'EM, GRANNY.

"Look at that old fool," Granny Ed nudged and whispered to me as she spied Old Emil waving his sign; yet I noticed a smile of satisfaction on her face from the show of support.

The buzzer sounded to start the game. Granny Ed slowly looked around the circle of ballplayers.

"Well, gentlemen, this is it! This is the big one we've been waiting to play. It's the whole ball of wax this time." She gave us a big wink and added, "Don't forget, I've got my secret weapon." And she pointed to the knitting needle neatly tucked in her braids.

I won't say the Orolatch team was tall. Let's put it this way. I'm six-feet, three-inches tall, and it strained my neck to look up at the forward I was to guard. The center opposite Al looked like Paul Bunyan's cousin, and I had the feeling that if he landed on Al, we would find only a splat on the floor where Al had once been. Such were the odds when the Lewisville Raiders played the Orolatch Tigers.

The team managed to stay even with Orolatch due to our fantastic shooting percentage during the first half. Leftie proved to be a deadeye, and we trailed by only two points at the end of the third quarter. The noise was terrific, and the tension was thick enough to cut. The fact that fouls were not being called closely added to the chaos. Al looked as though he'd been through a meat grinder. The big Orolatch center had worked him over with his elbows and knees.

I glanced at the bench and noticed Granny Ed was getting kind of purple-red in the face. The last straw was when the Orolatch center, driving to the basket, knocked Al flat, and the referee called the foul on Al who was lying on the floor.

"Basket counts!" the referee yelled, "and a foul on number twenty-three." A flash of red tennis shoes streaked toward the surprised referee. The rest I wish I could forget.

"Sir, and I use that term loosely," Granny Ed shouted, glaring angrily up at the face of the referee, "I brought a team on the floor to play basketball, not to have them dismembered. That asinine call only strengthens my belief that you are blind!" And with that she stripped her wire-framed glasses from her face and handed them to the dumbfounded referee.

There was a dead silence as he stared in disbelief at the small, gray-haired figure marching back to the Lewisville bench. Then it happened!

"Technical foul on the Raider bench!" he shouted, making the dreaded T sign with his hands and pointing straight at Granny Ed.

The big center missed his foul shots, but the Orolatch guard calmly stepped to the line and sank the technical. I looked up at the scoreboard. Two minutes in the game and Orolatch led 75–70. Well, we came close, I thought.

The Orolatch coach called timeout. It was pretty obvious what his strategy would be with only two minutes left.

"They will no doubt go into a stall," Granny Ed said. "Our only chance is to press and press hard. We've got to get possession of that ball!"

Leftie stole the out-of-bounds play and streaked the full length of the court for a lay-in. The crowd erupted with a deafening roar.

This time the Orolatch team passed the ball inbounds and were able to stall for a minute and a half before Al fouled the big center in a frantic try for the ball.

The big center swaggered to the foul line. His shot rolled round and round the rim and off. I timed my jump for the rebound perfectly, and that's the last thing I remember. The big guy had crashed into me. How I held the ball is a miracle, for I was sure my head must be lying somewhere underneath the basket.

"You hurt Sprout?" Granny Ed's voice was anxious as she bent over me on the floor. I shook my head feebly, although I wasn't sure all my body parts were still connected.

"All right then," she whispered in my ear, "you've got a one and one foul shot coming up, and we have no timeouts left. Make the first one and miss the second one. Al will rebound and score a field goal. There are only nine seconds left. Do you understand?"

I nodded weakly. Understand! Understand! Just like that I was to make the first free throw. There was a small matter of my being only a .500 freethrow shooter. Had Granny Ed taken that into consideration? I motioned to Al as I dragged my bruised body to the opposite end of the gym. I whispered Granny Ed's wild game plan to him. He nodded matter-of-factly and stationed himself along the side of the basket.

Shaking my head to clear out the spinning wheels, I stepped to the foul line. "This is crazy," I thought. I see two baskets up there. Now which one shall I aim for? I chose the top one in my half-conscious state and carefully arched the ball upward.

Swish! Down through the net it sailed. The noise of the crowd seemed very far away. Now miss this one. Granny Ed's words cut through the fog in my brain. I aimed the ball for the rim of the basket, and then I did something I've never told anyone—not even Granny Ed. I closed my eyes—tight. I never saw what happened in those last hectic seconds, but I heard a shriek erupt from the Lewisville fans.

"Fouled in the act of shooting!" the referee croaked. Al had rebounded and scored the field goal. He was gently pushing me aside to shoot the one shot that could win the ball game. Pandemonium broke loose. We'd won! The unbelievable had happened! Lewisville had won the State Championship! The team lifted Granny Ed to their shoulders and marched triumphantly out on the floor. She waved happily to the Lewisville rooters. As the players set her down, she grabbed my arm and whispered, "Big Thor should have been here! He always loved the tough ones."

Then a weird thing happened. The lights in that huge Coliseum dimmed, flickered, and came back on.

Granny Ed winked at me and said confidently, "He knows." And do you know something? I'm not so sure he doesn't. ॐ

THE NOBLE EXPERIMENT

FROM *I NEVER HAD IT MADE*

JACKIE ROBINSON

AS TOLD TO ALFRED DUCKETT

In 1910 Branch Rickey was a coach for Ohio Wesleyan. The team went to South Bend, Indiana, for a game. The hotel management registered the coach and team but refused to assign a room to a black player named Charley Thomas. In those days college ball had a few black players. Mr. Rickey took the manager aside and said he would move the entire team to another hotel unless the black athlete was accepted. The threat was a bluff because he knew the other hotels also would have refused accommodations to a black man. While the hotel manager was thinking about the threat, Mr. Rickey came up with a compromise. He suggested a cot be put in his own room, which he would share with the unwanted guest. The hotel manager wasn't happy about the idea, but he gave in.

Years later Branch Rickey told the story of the misery of that black player to whom he had given a place to sleep. He remembered that Thomas couldn't sleep.

"He sat on that cot," Mr. Rickey said, "and was silent for a long time. Then he began to cry, tears he couldn't hold back. His whole body shook with emotion. I sat and watched him, not knowing what to do until he began tearing at one hand with the other—just as if he were trying to scratch the skin off his hands with his fingernails. I was alarmed. I asked him what he was trying to do to himself.

Jackie Robinson in the Dodgers'
Montreal farm club uniform

"'It's my hands,' he sobbed. 'They're black. If only they were white, I'd be as good as anybody then, wouldn't I, Mr. Rickey? If only they were white.'"

"Charley," Mr. Rickey said, "the day will come when they won't have to be white."

Thirty-five years later, while I was lying awake nights, frustrated, unable to see a future, Mr. Rickey, by now the president of the Dodgers, was also lying awake at night, trying to make up his mind about a new experiment.

He had never forgotten the agony of that black athlete. When he became a front-office executive in St. Louis, he had fought, behind the scenes, against the custom that consigned black spectators to the Jim Crow section[1] of the Sportsman's Park, later to become Busch Memorial Stadium. His pleas to change the rules were in vain. Those in power argued that if blacks were allowed a free choice of seating, white business would suffer.

Branch Rickey lost that fight, but when he became the boss of the Brooklyn Dodgers in 1943, he felt the time for equality in baseball had come. He knew that achieving it would be terribly difficult. There would be deep resentment, determined opposition, and perhaps even racial violence. He was convinced he was morally right, and he shrewdly sensed that making the game a truly national one would have healthy financial results. He took his case before the startled directors of the club, and using persuasive eloquence, he won the first battle in what would be a long and bitter campaign. He was voted permission to make the Brooklyn club the pioneer in bringing blacks into baseball.

▲ ▲ ▲

Winning his directors' approval was almost insignificant in contrast to the task which now lay ahead of the Dodger president. He made certain that word of his plans did not leak out, particularly to the press. Next, he had to find the ideal player for his project, which came to be called "Rickey's noble experiment." This player had to be one who could take abuse, name-calling, rejection by fans and sportswriters and by fellow players not only on opposing teams but on his own. He had to be able to stand up in the face of merciless persecution and not retaliate. On the

---

1 **Jim Crow section:** the seats in the stadium where African-Americans were forced to sit

other hand, he had to be a contradiction in human terms; he still had to have spirit. He could not be an Uncle Tom.[2] His ability to turn the other cheek had to be predicated[3] on his determination to gain acceptance. Once having proven his ability as player, teammate, and man, he had to be able to cast off humbleness and stand up as a full-fledged participant whose triumph did not carry the poison of bitterness.

Unknown to most people and certainly to me, after launching a major scouting program, Branch Rickey had picked me as that player. The Rickey talent hunt went beyond national borders. Cuba, Mexico, Puerto Rico, Venezuela, and other countries where dark-skinned people lived had been checked out. Mr. Rickey had learned that there were a number of black players, war veterans mainly, who had gone to these countries, despairing of finding an opportunity in their own country. The manhunt had to be camouflaged. If it became known he was looking for a black recruit for the Dodgers, there would have been all kinds of trouble. The gimmick he used as a coverup was to make the world believe that he was about to establish a new Negro league. In the spring of 1945 he called a press conference and announced that the Dodgers were organizing the United States League, composed of all black teams. This, of course, made blacks and pro-integration whites indignant. He was accused of trying to uphold the existing segregation and, at the same time, capitalize on black players. Cleverly, Mr. Rickey replied that his league would be better organized than the current ones. He said its main purpose, eventually, was to be absorbed into the majors. It is ironic that by coming very close to telling the truth, he was able to conceal that truth from the enemies of integrated baseball. Most people assumed that when he spoke of some distant goal of integration, Mr. Rickey was being a hypocrite on this issue as so many of baseball's leaders had been.

Black players were familiar with this kind of hypocrisy. When I was with the Monarchs,[4] shortly before I met Mr. Rickey, Wendell Smith, then sports editor of the black, weekly Pittsburgh *Courier*, had arranged for me and two other players

2 **Uncle Tom:** a black person who tries to please white people; the term comes from Harriet Beecher Stowe's novel *Uncle Tom's Cabin*

3 **predicated:** based

4 **Monarchs:** the Kansas City Monarchs, a Negro League baseball team

from the Negro league to go to a tryout with the Boston Red Sox. The tryout had been brought about because a Boston city councilman had frightened the Red Sox management. Councilman Isadore Muchneck threatened to push a bill through banning Sunday baseball unless the Red Sox hired black players. Sam Jethroe of the Cleveland Buckeyes, Marvin Williams of the Philadelphia Stars, and I had been grateful to Wendell for getting us a chance in the Red Sox tryout, and we put our best efforts into it. However, not for one minute did we believe the try-out was sincere. The Boston club officials praised our performance, let us fill out application cards, and said "So long." We were fairly certain they wouldn't call us, and we had no intention of calling them.

Incidents like this made Wendell Smith as cynical as we were. He didn't accept Branch Rickey's new league as a genuine project, and he frankly told him so. During this conversation, the Dodger boss asked Wendell whether any of the three of us who had gone to Boston was really good major league material. Wendell said I was. I will be forever indebted to Wendell because, without his even knowing it, his recommendation was in the end partly responsible for my career. At the time, it started a thorough investigation of my background.

▲　▲　▲

In August 1945, at Comiskey Park in Chicago, I was approached by Clyde Sukeforth, the Dodger scout. Blacks have had to learn to protect themselves by being cynical but not cynical enough to slam the door on potential opportunities. We go through life walking a tightrope to prevent too much disillusionment. I was out on the field when Sukeforth called my name and beckoned. He told me the Brown Dodgers were looking for top ballplayers, that Branch Rickey had heard about me and sent him to watch me throw from the hole.[5] He had come at an unfortunate time. I had hurt my shoulder a couple of days before that, and I wouldn't be doing any throwing for at least a week.

Sukeforth said he'd like to talk with me anyhow. He asked me to come to see him after the game at the Stevens Hotel.

Here we go again, I thought. Another time-wasting experience. But Sukeforth looked like a sincere person, and I thought I might as well listen. I agreed to meet him that night. When we met, Sukeforth got right to the point. Mr. Rickey wanted to talk to me about the possibility

5 **throw from the hole:** throw from deep in the infield to first base

of becoming a Brown Dodger. If I could get a few days off and go to Brooklyn, my fare and expenses would be paid. At first I said that I couldn't leave my team and go to Brooklyn just like that. Sukeforth wouldn't take no for an answer. He pointed out that I couldn't play for a few days anyhow because of my bum arm. Why should my team object?

I continued to hold out and demanded to know what would happen if the Monarchs fired me. The Dodger scout replied quietly that he didn't believe that would happen.

I shrugged and said I'd make the trip. I figured I had nothing to lose.

Branch Rickey was an impressive-looking man. He had a classic face, an air of command, a deep, booming voice, and a way of cutting through red tape and getting down to basics. He shook my hand vigorously and, after a brief conversation, sprang the first question.

"You got a girl?" he demanded.

It was a heck of a question. I had two reactions: why should he be concerned about my relationship with a girl; and, second, while I thought, hoped, and prayed I had a girl, the way things had been going, I was afraid she might have begun to consider me a hopeless case. I explained this to Mr. Rickey and Clyde.

Mr. Rickey wanted to know all about Rachel. I told him of our hopes and plans.

"You know, you *have* a girl," he said heartily. "When we get through today, you may want to call her up because there are times when a man needs a woman by his side."

My heart began racing a little faster again as I sat there speculating. First he asked me if I really understood why he had sent for me. I told him what Clyde Sukeforth had told me.

"That's what he was supposed to tell you," Mr. Rickey said. "The truth is you are not a candidate for the Brooklyn Brown Dodgers. I've sent for you because I'm interested in you as a candidate for the Brooklyn National League Club. I think you can play in the major leagues. How do you feel about it?"

My reactions seemed like some kind of weird mixture churning in a blender. I was thrilled, scared, and excited. I was incredulous. Most of all, I was speechless.

"You think you can play for Montreal?" he demanded.

I got my tongue back. "Yes," I answered.

Montreal was the Brooklyn Dodgers' top farm club. The players who went there and made it had an excellent chance at the big time.

I was busy reorganizing my thoughts while Mr. Rickey and Clyde Sukeforth discussed me briefly, almost as if I weren't there. Mr. Rickey was questioning Clyde. Could I make the grade?

Abruptly, Mr. Rickey swung his swivel chair in my direction. He was a man who conducted himself with great drama. He pointed a finger at me.

"I know you're a good ballplayer," he barked. "What I don't know is whether you have the guts."

I knew it was all too good to be true. Here was a guy questioning my courage. That virtually amounted to him asking me if I was a coward. Mr. Rickey or no Mr. Rickey, that was an insinuation hard to take. I felt the heat coming up into my cheeks.

Before I could react to what he had said, he leaned forward in his chair and explained.

I wasn't just another athlete being hired by a ball club. We were playing for big stakes. This was the reason Branch Rickey's search had been so exhaustive. The search had spanned the globe and narrowed down to a few candidates, then finally to me. When it looked as though I might be the number-one choice, the investigation of my life, my habits, my reputation, and my character had become an intensified study.

"I've investigated you thoroughly, Robinson," Mr. Rickey said.

One of the results of this thorough screening were reports from California athletic circles that I had been a "racial agitator" at UCLA. Mr. Rickey had not accepted these criticisms on face value. He had demanded and received more information and came to the conclusion that if I had been white, people would have said, "Here's a guy who's a contender, a competitor."

After that he had some grim words of warning. "We can't fight our way through this, Robinson. We've got no army. There's virtually nobody on our side. No owners, no umpires, very few newspapermen. And I'm afraid that many fans will be hostile. We'll be in a tough position. We can win only if we can convince the world that I'm doing this because you're a great ballplayer and a fine gentleman."

He had me transfixed as he spoke. I could feel his sincerity, and I began to get a sense of how much this major step meant to him. Because of his nature and his passion for justice, he had to do what he was doing. He continued. The rumbling voice, the theatrical gestures, were gone. He was speaking from a deep, quiet strength.

"So there's more than just playing," he said. "I wish it meant only hits,

Robinson with Brooklyn Dodger president, Branch Rickey

runs, and errors—only the things they put in the box score. Because you know—yes, you would know, Robinson, that a baseball box score is a democratic thing. It doesn't tell how big you are, what church you attend, what color you are, or how your father voted in the last election. It just tells what kind of baseball player you were on that particular day."

I interrupted. "But it's the box score that really counts—that and that alone, isn't it?"

"It's all that *ought* to count," he replied. "But it isn't. Maybe one of these days it *will* be all that counts. That is one of the reasons I've got you here, Robinson. If you're a good enough man, we can make this a start in the right direction. But let me tell you, it's going to take an awful lot of courage."

He was back to the crossroads question that made me start to get angry minutes earlier. He asked it slowly and with great care.

"Have you got the guts to play the game no matter what happens?"

"I think I can play the game, Mr. Rickey," I said.

The next few minutes were tough. Branch Rickey had to make absolutely sure that I knew what I would face. Beanballs[6] would be thrown at me. I would be called the kind of names which would hurt and infuriate any man. I would be physically attacked. Could I take all of this and control my temper, remain steadfastly loyal to our ultimate aim?

He knew I would have terrible problems and wanted me to know the extent of them before I agreed to the plan. I was twenty-six years old, and all my life—back to the age of eight when a little neighbor girl called

6 **beanballs:** baseballs thrown on purpose at the batter's head

me a nigger—I had believed in payback, retaliation. The most luxurious possession, the richest treasure anybody has, is his personal dignity. I looked at Mr. Rickey guardedly, and in that second I was looking at him not as a partner in a great experiment, but as the enemy—a white man. I had a question, and it was the age-old one about whether or not you sell your birthright.

"Mr. Rickey," I asked, "are you looking for a Negro who is afraid to fight back?"

I never will forget the way he exploded.

"Robinson," he said, "I'm looking for a ballplayer with guts enough not to fight back."

After that, Mr. Rickey continued his lecture on the kind of thing I'd be facing.

He not only told me about it, but he acted out the part of a white player charging into me, blaming me for the "accident" and calling me all kinds of foul racial names. He talked about my race, my parents, in language that was almost unendurable.

"They'll taunt and goad you," Mr. Rickey said. "They'll do anything to make you react. They'll try to provoke a race riot in the ballpark. This is the way to prove to the public that a Negro should not be allowed in the major league. This is the way to frighten the fans and make them afraid to attend the games."

If hundreds of black people wanted to come to the ballpark to watch me play and Mr. Rickey tried to discourage them, would I understand that he was doing it because the emotional enthusiasm of my people could harm the experiment? That kind of enthusiasm would be as bad as the emotional opposition of prejudiced white fans.

Suppose I was at shortstop. Another player comes down from first, stealing, flying in with spikes high, and cuts me on the leg. As I feel the blood running down my leg, the white player laughs in my face.

"How do you like that, nigger boy?" he sneers.

Could I turn the other cheek? I didn't know how I would do it. Yet I knew that I must. I had to do it for so many reasons. For black youth, for my mother, for Rae, for myself. I had already begun to feel I had to do it for Branch Rickey.

I was offered, and agreed to sign later, a contract with a $3,500 bonus and a $600-a-month salary. I was officially a Montreal Royal. I must not tell anyone except Rae and my mother. ∾

WALKING AWAY,
WHILE HE STILL CAN

IRA BERKOW

PULLMAN, WASHINGTON—Timm Rosenbach remembers clearly the beginning of the end because everything was pitch black.

He woke up in a dark room with his head strapped to a table, still wearing his Phoenix Cardinals uniform and shoulder pads and hip pads and cleats. He was frightened and alone, not sure if he was alive or dead. He couldn't move, didn't want to move. He knew he had been hurt, but didn't know how badly. He thought about his friend and former college teammate, Mike Utley of the Lions, who the year before had taken a tumble in a game and been left paralyzed for life from the chest down.

Then Rosenbach remembered the hit he had taken earlier that day. Was it minutes ago? Was it hours? Rosenbach, a six-foot quarterback, was dropping back to pass in the third quarter of the season opener when he was blindsided by Santana Dodson, the Tampa Bay Buccaneers' six-foot-five, 270-pound defensive end, in one of the brutal encounters that is commonplace in a National Football League game.

Rosenbach remembered only the resounding impact, as if being leveled by a tank, and then nothing. Until that moment in the room. And then, just as suddenly, he blacked out again.

This was Sunday, September 6, 1992, in an X-ray room at St. Joseph's Hospital in Phoenix. Rosenbach was not aware that he had been taken, unmoving, from the field at Sun Devils Stadium on a stretcher and rushed to the emergency room. He was not aware that he had suffered only a severe concussion when his head slammed into the turf.

He would walk and talk normally again, even report back for work two days later, but the grim experience would not leave him. In the following game, he returned to the lineup only to be blindsided again, this time by Clyde Simmons, Philadelphia's six-foot-six, 280-pound defensive end, on the Cardinals' second series of the game.

"I made sure that the next time I get hit, I don't go head first," Rosenbach recalled, "and I didn't. I went shoulder first." And he suffered a separated shoulder. He was out of action for a month.

After the last game of the season, December 27, 1992, Rosenbach, at age twenty-six, did what some thought was unthinkable: He walked away from professional football and $1.05 million, the salary for the fifth and last year of his $5.3 million contract. He left the field and the money because he had developed fears that he might be crippled if he continued to play and because he began to "despise," as he said, the dehumanizing aspects of football that "can turn you into an animal."

It wasn't always that way. Two years earlier, in 1990, in his second year in the NFL, he took every snap for the Cardinals, all 1,001 of them, throwing for 3,098 yards to rank third in the National Football Conference. He ranked second in the NFL in rushing yardage[1] for a quarterback, behind Randall Cunningham. He threw 16 touchdown passes. He was admired, as one Phoenix sports reporter wrote, because, "He was feisty. Gutsy. Combative. Ornery." His coach, Joe Bugel, called him "a throwback," a "gun-slingin' beer-drinkin' tough" in the mold of the late and colorful Bobby Layne.[2]

When it became apparent that Rosenbach had made his decision to quit football and return to Washington State University—where he had starred in football and where he was thirty-eight hours short of a bachelor's degree in general studies with an emphasis in psychology—he didn't call the team. His agent, Gary Wichard, did. Rosenbach changed his unlisted phone number so that no one from the Cardinals organization could call to try to talk him out of retiring and no reporter could call and ask why.

Football generally had been fun for Rosenbach in school, and even into the pros—he once relished the contact, proudly looking in the mirror at

1 **rushing yardage:** number of yards accumulated by running down the field with the football

2 **Bobby Layne:** Hall of Fame quarterback who played from 1948-1962. He played for the Chicago Bears, the New York Bulldogs, the Detroit Lions, and the Pittsburgh Steelers.

his bruises as an affirmation[3] of manhood. But he was not prepared, as a 22-year-old right out of college, for the hard-edged business of professional football, nor for the debilitating[4] injuries that had sidelined him. And while his associations with a number of his teammates remained close, his view of this odd occupation became deeper, and darker.

There was speculation that Rosenbach had decided to become a professional rodeo rider, since he had participated as a team roper in a half-dozen events. When he married Carrie Serrano in June 1992, at his new 10-acre ranch in Gilbert, Arizona, the ceremony was held outdoors under a sagebrush arch with groom and groomsmen bedecked in black cowboy hats, tuxedo tops, black jeans and black cowboy boots.

"It's all a mystery to me," said Bugel. "I'd like for him to tell me right to my face what the problem is."

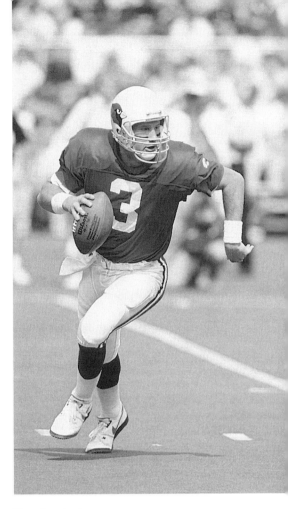

Timm Rosenbach

"I've seen young guys retire, unretire, but certainly not a player of Timm's stature," said Larry Wilson, the Cardinals' general manager. "This is kind of strange."

But there was more to it than just the bruises of the business. "I thought I was turning into some kind of animal," Rosenbach said in a recent interview. "You go through a week getting yourself up for a game by hating the other team, the other players. You're so mean and hateful, you want to kill somebody. Football's so aggressive. Things get done by force. And then you come home, you're supposed to turn it off? 'Oh, here's your lovin' daddy.' It's not that easy. It was like I was an idiot. I felt programmed. I had become a machine. I became sick of it."

3 **affirmation:** a positive feeling or assertion
4 **debilitating:** weakening

He remembered those "barbaric yawps,[5]" as he called them, when breaking from a huddle and the players began screaming like maniacs. "It lightened things up," said Rosenbach, "but it's still a part of the craziness of football. Like screaming at the other team at the top of your lungs all kinds of threats and obscenities."

He remembers his center, Bill Lewis, telling an opposing lineman, "You touch my quarterback and I'll end your career." He remembers players like Refrigerator Perry snarling with his huge face scrunched up inside his tight helmet. And then there was Reggie White: "He is very religious, and he'd hit you a murderous shot and then say, 'God bless you,' as he pulled you off the ground."

Rosenbach also felt the pressures that go with winning, or losing. "I began to despise the whole business of the NFL," he said. When he was injured, he felt that the coaches, particularly head coaches, hardly recognized him. Since he was of no value to them, he was a virtual nonentity.[6] When he was hurt, he wasn't even asked to travel with the team. "They asked, 'How're you feelin'?' But with no feeling," he said. "Their answer to injury is to give you painkiller pills. And the whole concept of medicine is to get you ready to perform—what happens to you down the road is not of any interest to them.

"Team doctors often lose touch with humanity, too. They are working for the team, and love the association. So you hear players on the plane after a game and saying, 'Hey, Doc, give me some Percodan or Percoset or Codeine Tylenol or something else.' When did players become pharmacists?

"And coaches are so absorbed in the X's and O's that they lose any feeling of being a human being. I guess the pressure is so great on them. I feel they viewed me—us—as robots. A mechanism. And if you don't fit the slot you're nothing to them."

▲ ▲ ▲

One trick of being a professional athlete, he understood, was not to think too much. He had been a kind of daredevil quarterback, enjoying the contact, loving that glazed feeling when you hardly know where you are, even baiting some of the huge opponents like Perry during the heat of a game—"It takes a long time to get all that into motion, doesn't it?"—but

5 **barbaric yawps:** unrecognizable yells or hoots

6 **nonentity:** a nobody; a person of no consequence

when he returned to the lineup in the latter part of the last season, things were different.

He couldn't move the way he used to because his knee was wrapped in a brace, and for the first time he felt fear on a football field, the fear of ending up a cripple. He had already missed the entire 1991 season because of a severed ligament incurred[7] in a preseason practice a week before the opener. The injury required reconstructive surgery and rehabilitation and made him question his existence as a pro football player.

The challenge of going against ferocious linemen like Lawrence Taylor and White and Simmons and Perry, which had whetted his competitive appetite, had taken a different turn.

He said there was a lot of fear in the NFL. "Guys don't talk about it," he said, "but they feel it. And when you really know the game, you can spot them. But a lot aren't making the kind of money I did. And when a guy's making, say, $65,000 a year, and this is the only place he can make that kind of money, he's not about to get out."

After the injuries, his confidence, as well as his enthusiasm ebbed noticeably. He was booed. He remembers the discomfort of meeting people and feeling he had to apologize for his performance or the team's losses.

"Timm would come home in these moods," said his wife, Carrie, "and we were newlyweds. I didn't know what the problem was. He'd sit in a dark corner. I thought it was me. I thought, 'Why can't I make him happy?' But then I began to understand all the pressures he was under. And of course the pain. After some games, Timm was so bruised and battered it would take him a half-hour to get out of bed. And sometimes it would take him a half-hour to get off the couch and into bed."

The other side of life in the NFL for Rosenbach was that of "royalty," as he describes it. In those earlier, more relaxed days, he felt pampered, and that it was his due.

"I had a lot of money—more than I ever dreamed—a great apartment, several cars, and wanted for nothing," he said. "I had become pretty arrogant. My neighbors hated me. I lived in an exclusive condominium in my first few years and played my music loud and didn't throw my garbage in the dumpster but left it on the porch.

"I almost never washed my clothes," he said. "When they got dirty, I threw them into the closet and went down to the mall and bought some

7 **incurred:** received

more. I was young and rich and a professional athlete and I had no sense of reality. Just like most of the rest of the guys I played with."

▲ ▲ ▲

Rosenbach's late father, Lynn, was a high school football coach and later the assistant athletic director at Washington State. His mother, Rosie, is an interior decorator. His brother, Todd, teaches special education, and his sister, Dana, is a high school teacher.

"When I went back and saw their lives," he said, "saw how they were all doing well on salaries that weren't a million dollars a year, and happy with their lives, I felt embarrassed for myself."

He spoke with Carrie about quitting and giving up that $1 million, as well as the millions that he might earn in football in the coming years.

"I didn't know how he could just give up all that money," said Carrie. "But after a while I understood. He said that if he had to pump gas, he'd do it rather than play football. And it was true."

In Phoenix, he was being called a "no-show," and a "mystery man."

But his agent, Gary Wichard, said: "Timm's an intelligent, sensitive guy, and he has made a decision that he's had it with football. He could have come in for a year and held for extra points and field goals, but that's just not Timm."

"I'm proud of Rosey," said Jim Wahler, a defensive lineman for the Redskins and a former Cardinal teammate of Rosenbach's. "I'm glad he did it. There are not many people in that position to do that. That's a standup thing to walk out on your own terms and not somebody else's. Most guys would like that opportunity."

He still has his ranch in Gilbert, but now lives with Carrie and seven dogs in a small house in an isolated area about eight miles outside of Pullman, Washington. She is a graduate of Arizona State and is in school at Washington State going for a master's degree in agricultural economy. Rosenbach has returned to general studies with a psychology emphasis.

Is he happier? "Yes," he said. "I was getting no enjoyment out of football anymore.

"It's funny, but when I was in school here before I sat in the back of the class and never said a word. Now I'm involved in the classes, and I'm always raising my hand. I'm sure some of the students are saying, 'Why doesn't that old guy just shut up?'"

Rosenbach hardly looks ancient in his sweatshirt and jeans. He still has that broad, boyish look and a cowlick in his short blond hair. And he also hasn't totally given up on football. He says a college game is still one of the exciting spectacles for him. And he still watches pro games on television, remembering the pleasure of the camaraderie of teammates, though he sees the action differently than he once did.

And he still has his memories of playing the game, every morning. His knees, his back, his shoulders, still ache when he wakes up and slowly gets out of bed. When he drives for any distance in his truck, or walks distances when he is out hunting birds, his body hurts.

"And I'm still an alumnus of the NFL, it is still something I'm proud of," he said. "And I guess one day I'll be invited to some of those alumni golf tournaments, and wear an NFL cap and play, if I can stand up." ∿

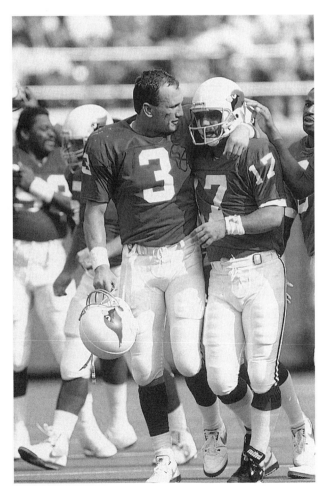

Rosenbach and teammate

RESPONDING TO CLUSTER THREE

IS WINNING EVERYTHING?

Thinking Skill   INFERRING

1. Write a **character sketch** of Granny Ed. Include details about her attitude toward winning, about her appearance, and about her relationship with her grandson and her players.

2. Use **inference** to determine what motives Branch Rickey and Jackie Robinson might have had for attempting to break baseball's color barrier. Use details from the article to support your inference.

3. In "The Noble Experiment" Branch Rickey says to Jackie Robinson, "I'm looking for a ballplayer with guts enough not to fight back." Compare Robinson to Timm Rosenbach in "Walking Away, While He Still Can." Who is the more courageous? Explain.

4. Write one sentence about each major character in this cluster that states his or her attitude toward winning.

Writing Activity: Is Winning Everything?

"Winning is not everything. It's the only thing."
—Hall of Fame football coach Vince Lombardi

"Winning after all is easy. It's losing that takes courage."
—former heavyweight champion Floyd Patterson

Choose one athlete from this cluster and, using facts from the selection, write an essay **inferring** how the athlete would react to either of the above statements.

A Strong Inference

• is based on facts, judgments, statements, or actions in a selection

• draws conclusions beyond the information presented

CLUSTER FOUR

Thinking On Your Own

Thinking Skill SYNTHESIZING

JAMEZ LYNCH, AGE 17

I play football in the fall, basketball in the winter, and soccer and track in the spring. It seems natural for me to do four varsity sports a year because I've been involved in team sports since before I was in school. I love the mental process both before and during the game as much as the physical challenge of the sport. While my teammates whoop and holler and get themselves all pumped up to play, I find myself getting quieter and quieter, going deep inside myself to find my concentration. The most important thing my coaches have taught me is that talent isn't as important as dedication. If you show up and work hard, good things will happen to you.

My grandma is probably my biggest fan both on and off the court. She took care of me when my mom was at school and at work and got me playing soccer when I was four. She's a teacher, so I've always had a lot of respect for grades. She always said if you do good in your books, you'll do the same in sports. The dedication and concentration is the same in the classroom and on the playing field. I made the honor roll this year and that means as much to me as the points I've scored in basketball. I don't want to be bagging groceries or pumping gas for the rest of my life. I want to go to college and get a good job—one that can support a family and that I'll enjoy. Sports are a ticket for me to get into college. I mean, I love playing to win, but it's more than a game. It can help me make a future for myself. Some kids think it's cool to be hard, walking around the school pimping and everything, skipping class and hanging out. One day those guys will be working for the kids that were going to school and playing sports. Who's cool then?

My high school is definitely run by different cliques. The separations aren't so much by racial lines as by different groups and organizations. I usually sit with my teammates in the cafeteria. You sit next to your friends in the classroom and it often turns out that all the black kids are on one side of the room and all the white kids are on the other side of the room. Kids are always afraid of being accused of trying to "act black" or "act white" and that's a real shame. It really makes me mad when black kids accuse me of "acting white" because I want to make good grades. Can't a black person be smart? It seems like black culture respects sports achievements most of all. At least in my generation, more kids admire Michael Jordan than Thurgood Marshall. Back when my parents were my age, it seems like there were more impressive black leaders. Where is the Martin Luther King or the Malcolm X of today? There's no public person—black or white—that kids today really admire except the sports heroes.

When my friends and I walk down the street, you can tell it makes people nervous. Every time you see a young black male in the news or on TV, they're usually committing a crime. If you go to school and hold down a weekend job like I do, you don't hear much about it. The news tells all about the twenty black guys that jumped some poor white guy because he was trying to go to a store in their neighborhood. I guess kids like me are just not news, but that doesn't mean we don't exist, that we're less "real" than a gangsta. The headline is some kid shooting another kid and the girl that gets a perfect score on her SATs gets a little tiny mention in the back of the paper.

I hope to get a scholarship to an out-of-state school, because I'd like to experience other places. It's a big world out there and I'd like to check it out. My family, teachers, coaches and minister have taught me a lot over the years and someday soon I'd like to try the world on my own. I guess college is a good first step. ∾

Jamez Lynch

CAM POWELL, AGE 16

I just had my sixteenth birthday last week. I got my own surfboard at nine and used my older friends' boards before that. I had a friend whose dad was a surfer and he'd take us with him all the time. By the time I turned ten, I was competing in contests. I placed pretty well right away, so after just a few contests, I got sponsored by a local surfboard company and started competing regularly, usually getting firsts, so I decided to go on to bigger contests and started traveling up and down the East Coast, competing from New York to Florida.

This summer I was in five contests in California. Rusty surfboards and clothing and Oakley sunglasses, along with 17th Street Surf Shop, help me with my traveling expenses and entry fees. I made my first surf trip to Costa Rica with my brother when I was thirteen and loved the great waves in a tropical environment. I went back in February with a couple of friends and we traveled all over both coasts this time. If I wasn't doing home school, I'd be

Cam Powell

starting my sophomore year. Some school in Nebraska develops my curriculum. They send me all my books, schedules and deadlines and even send people to my house from time to time to make sure I'm learning. There's a professional surfer on the circuit who oversees my tests, but otherwise it's pretty much up to me to get my work done.

I think I can get along with adults much better than most kids my age, because I'm not so isolated from grown-ups as kids who are sitting together in school all day. High school is kind of a teenage ghetto. I'm fortunate to have friends of all different ages because of my surfing.

For me, surfing is not just a sport, it's a whole way of life. I definitely wouldn't be who I am if I didn't surf. It's the number one thing in my life. In big waves, like we had in Mexico, your heart gets pumping, not from paddling, but because you fear for your life. A thirty foot wave is pretty humbling. You can't wear a leash in waves that size, because if you fall, the waves are so powerful, they'll rip your leg off. You've got to be in terrific shape to surf competitively or in big waves. Me and my friends don't ever smoke cigarettes or pot and only rarely drink—never before a contest. I definitely have a healthier lifestyle because of my love for the sport. Most of us eat healthy food and work out for that competitive edge. Sure there's the surfers that lead a real degenerate lifestyle, but they get left behind, and that's not where I want to be. I'm not sure, really, why surfers have such a bad reputation. I mean, most of us are not reeling around stoned going "What's up, dude?" I don't know one single person like that. I think our relationship with the beach and the ocean makes us more concerned about the environment than the average kid.

Pretty much wherever you pollute, it's going to go into the ocean. If you throw trash on the street, it ends up in the storm drain and eventually makes its way to the sea. I don't even spit gum on the ground, because I hate stepping in it. If there's any trash on the beach, I pick it up. It's a surfer thing to leave the beach cleaner than it was when we got there. I got a fungus on my face from surfing in dirty water in California. It's gross. We've got to protect our oceans. It's insane that the storm drains flow untreated into our oceans or that cities haul their garbage out to sea. ❧

THE DECLINE OF SPORT

(A PREPOSTEROUS PARABLE)

E. B. WHITE

E.B. White wrote this essay during the 1950s to predict what professional sports might be like 30 years later. His gaze into the crystal ball seems eerily accurate.

In the third decade of the supersonic age, sport gripped the nation in an ever-tightening grip. The horse tracks, the ballparks, the fight rings, the gridirons, all drew crowds in steadily increasing numbers. Every time a game was played, an attendance record was broken. Usually some other sort of record was broken, too—such as the record for the number of consecutive doubles hit by left-handed batters in a Series game, or some such thing as that. Records fell like ripe apples on a windy day. Customs and manners changed, and the five-day business week was reduced to four days, then to three, to give everyone a better chance to memorize the scores.

Not only did sport proliferate[1] but the demands it made on the spectator became greater. Nobody was content to take in one event at a time, and thanks to the magic of radio and television nobody had to. A Yale alumnus,[2] class of 1962, returning to the Bowl with 197,000 others to see the Yale-Cornell football game would take along his pocket radio and pick up the Yankee Stadium, so that while his eye might be following a fumble on the Cornell twenty-two-yard line, his ear would be following a

---

1 **proliferate:** increase in number
2 **alumnus:** a graduate

man going down to second in the top of the fifth, seventy miles away. High in the blue sky above the Bowl, skywriters would be at work writing the scores of other major and minor sporting contests, weaving an interminable[3] record of victory and defeat, and using the new high-visibility pink news-smoke perfected by Pepsi-Cola engineers. And in the frames of the giant video sets, just behind the goalposts, this same alumnus could watch Dejected win the Futurity before a record-breaking crowd of 349,872 at Belmont, each of whom was tuned to the Yale Bowl and following the World Series game in the video and searching the sky for further news of events either under way or just completed. The effect of this vast cyclorama[4] of sport was to divide the spectator's attention, oversubtilize[5] his appreciation, and deaden his passion. As the fourth supersonic decade was ushered in, the picture changed and sport began to wane.

A good many factors contributed to the decline of sport. Substitutions in football had increased to such an extent that there were very few fans in the United States capable of holding the players in mind during play. Each play that was called saw two entirely new elevens lined up, and the players whose names and faces you had familiarized yourself with in the first period were seldom seen or heard of again. The spectacle became as diffuse[6] as the main concourse in Grand Central at the commuting hour.[7]

Express motor highways leading to the parks and stadia[8] had become so wide, so unobstructed, so devoid of all life except automobiles and trees that sport fans had got into the habit of travelling enormous distances to attend events. The normal driving speed had been stepped up to ninety-five miles an hour, and the distance between cars had been decreased to fifteen feet. This put an extraordinary strain on the sport lover's nervous system, and he arrived home from a Saturday game, after a road trip of three hundred and fifty miles, glassy-eyed, dazed, and spent. He hadn't really had any relaxation and he had failed to see Czlika

3 **interminable:** unending

4 **cyclorama:** image or screen that completely surrounds the spectator; here it means a confusing spectacle

5 **oversubtilize:** refine

6 **diffuse:** disorganized

7 **the main concourse in Grand Central...:** very crowded and confusing; easy to lose track of someone

8 **stadia:** plural of *stadium*

(who had gone in for Trusky) take the pass from Bkeco (who had gone in for Bjallo) in the third period, because at that moment a youngster named Lavagetto had been put in to pinch-hit for Art Gurlack in the bottom of the ninth with the tying run on second, and the skywriter who was attempting to write "Princeton 0–Lafayette 43" had banked the wrong way, muffed the "3," and distracted everyone's attention from the fact that Lavagetto had been whiffed.[9]

Cheering, of course, lost its stimulating effect on players, because cheers were no longer associated necessarily with the immediate scene but might as easily apply to something that was happening somewhere else. This was enough to infuriate even the steadiest performer. A football star, hearing the stands break into a roar before the ball was snapped, would realize that their minds were not on him, and would become dispirited and grumpy. Two or three of the big coaches worried so about this that they considered equipping all players with tiny ear sets, so that they, too, could keep abreast of other sporting events while playing, but the idea was abandoned as impractical, and the coaches put it aside in tickler files,[10] to bring up again later.

I think the event that marked the turning point in sport and started it downhill was the Midwest's classic Dust Bowl game of 1975, when Eastern Reserve's great right end, Ed Pistachio, was shot by a spectator. This man, the one who did the shooting, was seated well down in the stands near the forty-yard line on a bleak October afternoon and was so saturated with sport and with the disappointments of sport that he had clearly become deranged. With a minute and fifteen seconds to play and the score tied, the Eastern Reserve quarterback had whipped a long pass over Army's heads into Pistachio's waiting arms. There was no other player anywhere near him, and all Pistachio had to do was catch the ball and run it across the line. He dropped it. At exactly this moment, the spectator—a man named Homer T. Parkinson, of 35 Edgemere Drive, Toledo, O.—suffered at least three other major disappointments in the realm of sport. His horse, Hiccough, on which he had a five-hundred-dollar bet, fell while getting away from the starting gate at Pimlico and broke its leg (clearly visible in the video); his favorite shortstop, Lucky Frimstitch, struck out and let three men die on base in the final game of the Series (to which Parkinson was tuned); and the Governor Dummer

9 **whiffed:** struck out

10 **tickler files:** files that hold information to be remembered later

soccer team, on which Parkinson's youngest son played goalie, lost to Kent, 4–3, as recorded in the sky overhead. Before anyone could stop him, he drew a gun and drilled Pistachio, before 954,000 persons, the largest crowd that had ever attended a football game and the *second*-largest crowd that had ever assembled for any sporting event in any month except July.

This tragedy, by itself, wouldn't have caused sport to decline, I suppose, but it set in motion a chain of other tragedies, the cumulative[11] effect of which was terrific. Almost as soon as the shot was fired, the news flash was picked up by one of the skywriters directly above the field. He glanced down to see whether he could spot the trouble below, and in doing so failed to see another skywriter approaching. The two planes collided and fell, wings locked, leaving a confusing trail of smoke, which some observers tried to interpret as a late sports score. The planes struck in the middle of the nearby eastbound coast-to-coast Sunlight Parkway, and a motorist driving a convertible coupé stopped so short, to avoid hitting them, that he was bumped from behind. The pileup of cars that ensued involved 1,482 vehicles, a record for eastbound parkways. A total of more than three thousand persons lost their lives in the highway accident, including the two pilots, and when panic broke out in the stadium, it cost another 872 in dead and injured. News of the disaster spread quickly to other sports arenas, and started other panics among the crowds trying to get to the exits, where they could buy a paper and study a list of the dead. All in all, the afternoon of sport cost 20,003 lives, a record. And nobody had much to show for it except one small Midwestern boy who hung around the smoking wrecks of the planes, captured some aero news-smoke in a milk bottle, and took it home as a souvenir.

From that day on, sport waned. Through long, noncompetitive Saturday afternoons, the stadia slumbered. Even the parkways fell into disuse as motorists rediscovered the charms of old, twisty roads that led through main streets and past barnyards, with their mild congestions and pleasant smells. ∾

11 **cumulative:** total

A QUIET WEDDING

WILLIAM HAZLETT UPSON

On Thursday afternoon, in the front office of the Coliseum at Prairie City, Iowa, Bill Bozeman, three-hundred pound black-bearded professional wrestler, was conferring with his manager, a buxom and highly efficient young woman by the name of Miss Bella Jones, who a few years previously had abandoned her career as a circus bareback rider to devote her peculiar talents to the commercial side of the professional wrestling game. Bill and Bella were discussing their approaching marriage.

"What I want," Bill said, "is just a simple, quiet wedding."

"What you're going to have," Bella said, "is an elaborate, noisy brawl—with plenty of vulgar excitement, and as big a mob as we can drag in. It's a wonderful chance to put over a lot of swell publicity."

"Maybe so," Bill said. "And I don't mind publicity about my wrestling. But when we're getting married, I figure it is our own personal business. So what we want is just a nice quiet—"

"Listen," said Bella. "Before you took me on as your manager you were just a ham. Now you're the best box-office attraction in the Middle West. And what did it? Publicity!"

"Not entirely," Bill said. "Don't forget that I'm a pretty good wrestler."

"I know it. But it isn't straight wrestling that brings in the cash customers. You've built yourself up as a swell drawing card by following my advice and giving the fans a good show—wearing those whiskers and billing yourself as the Bearded Behemoth, roaring and snarling and tearing around the ring like a drunken gorilla, and pulling off stunts like that fight out in the street last week and so on."

"Well," Bill said, "I still got my beard. I can still roar when I'm in the ring. And if you want, I could stage another street fight."

"No," Bella said. "That's old stuff now. We got to give them something new. And this wedding is just the chance we need. So I've figured out a setup that will just naturally drive the fans crazy."

"And just what are you planning to do?" asked Bill, suspiciously.

"I'm announcing that I can't make up my mind whether to marry you or Clarence Alford. So it's going to be decided by the wrestling match next Saturday night. Whichever one of you wins gets me as a prize."

"What! You mean you'd actually consider marrying that low-down, chicken-livered ex-acrobat, Clarence Alford?"

"Certainly not," snorted Bella. "I'm working out the scenario for the bout so Clarence will almost get you, but you'll flatten him in the end."

"We don't need any scenario for that," said Bill, indignantly.[1] "I can flatten that rat any time I feel like it."

"All right," said Bella. "So after you've won the bout, we'll have the wedding right there in the ring. I'm going to have a full brass band—"

"I won't stand for it," said Bill.

"You've got to," said Bella. "It is all decided. And here's the advance publicity." She flashed a copy of the Prairie City Evening Times. With growing indignation Bill read the following item:

GRUNT AND GROAN BOYS EMULATE KNIGHTS OF OLD —JOUST FOR HAND OF FAIR LADY

"Just as the plumed knights of yore were wont to engage in deadly combat for the hand of some fair lady, so two mighty gladiators of today, Clarence Alford, the Akron (Ohio) Adonis, and Bill Bozeman, the Bearded Behemoth, will clash in a bitterly contested wrestling bout on Saturday evening at the local Coliseum to decide which is to win the hand in marriage of Miss Bella Jones, beautiful and attractive local business girl.

"When interviewed this afternoon, Miss Jones expressed her warm regard for the Akron Adonis, who is renowned from coast to coast for his beautifully developed body, for his clean sportsmanship, and for his gentlemanly tactics in the ring. On the other hand, Miss Jones admitted that she is deeply fascinated by the sheer brute power, and the animal cruelty of the hideously hairy Bearded Behemoth. Unable to choose between the curiously

---

1 **indignantly:** angrily

contrasting charms of these two ardent suitors,[2] she says she has decided to stake her entire future on the outcome of the wrestling match to be held next Saturday night.

"The exact motives underlying Miss Jones's strange decision are the subject of considerable discussion by local psychologists. It is possible that she may be honestly and sincerely bewildered when she attempts to evaluate the relative charms of her two manly lovers, and that she has hit upon this wrestling match as the only possible means of solving the dilemma which tears her now this way, now that. On the other hand there are many who charge that she is actuated[3] by overweening pride and selfish vanity—by a neurotic craving for the thrill that will come when she witnesses this epic battle, and realizes that these mighty men are fighting for her, and her alone.

"In any event, the general delectability and oomph possessed by the prize are sure to inspire a battle of unprecedented and blood-curdling ferocity. The customers are certain to get their money's worth."

As Bill finished reading, Bella smiled proudly. "What do you think of it?" she asked.

"It's a bunch of tripe,"[4] said Bill. "I don't see how these sporting writers can produce such stuff."

"They can't," said Bella. "They haven't the ability. I wrote the whole thing myself."

"I still say it's tripe," said Bill. "And I bet Sammy Ringo will agree with me." Sammy Ringo was the owner of the Coliseum and producer of the wrestling bouts.

"I explained the whole thing to Sammy yesterday," said Bella. "He thought it was swell. He told me to go ahead. And he's the boss around here, so what he says goes. You know that."

"Just the same, I don't like it, and I won't stand for it. Have you told Clarence yet?"

"Yes."

"What did he say?"

"Oh, he had a lot of childish objections. He said in the first place he didn't like me, and in the second place he had a wife already, so he couldn't pretend he wanted to marry me."

2 **suitors:** men who seek to marry a woman

3 **actuated:** moved

4 **tripe:** something worthless or offensive

"And what did you say to that?"

"I told him I wouldn't marry him for a million dollars because I like him even less than he doesn't like me—and he doesn't have to worry about his wife, because he hasn't lived with her for years, and she is way back east in Newark, New Jersey, or some such place, where she won't even hear about this business. And, finally, I told him it was all according to orders from Sammy Ringo himself, so Clarence had to agree—just the way you're going to agree."

"I'll never agree," said Bill. "What I want is just a nice quiet—"

"I'm sorry," interrupted Bella, "but I got no time to argue. I got to go and work up some more publicity."

The next day—Friday—the local paper carried another article playing up the coming wrestling bout and wedding. There was also a letter to the editor, as follows:

"TO THE EDITOR OF THE *TIMES*. Sir:—For some time past the more thoughtful members of the community have viewed with alarm the increasing wave of indecency and loose-living which seems to be sweeping across this country. Those of us who wish to preserve the sanctity of the American home and the purity of American womanhood have stood aghast at the inroads being made by the forces of communism, nazism, atheism, companionship marriage, free love, Trojan horses, easy divorce, birth control, selfishness, greed, irreverence, the liquor traffic, gambling, and the so-called freedom of the younger generation. But the climax of all these iniquitous[5] movements is reached in the shocking performance announced in today's paper. I refer to the so-called wrestling match which is planned for Saturday night at the Coliseum, where, according to your paper, some shameless hussy—I will not dignify her by the name of woman—is brazenly[6] offering her body as a prize to the victor of a brutal and degrading physical combat. In the name of common decency I call upon you, Mr. Editor, to exclude from your columns all further publicity and advertising for this affair, and, in the name of the law, I call upon the police of Prairie City to stop this degenerate spectacle. (Signed) Outraged Womanhood."

Bill showed the letter to Bella.

"This shows," he said, "what we're getting into by exploiting ourselves this way. I don't like it. I won't stand for people calling you a—what was

5 **iniquitous:** wicked
6 **brazenly:** with disrespect

it, now?" He looked over the letter again. "Oh, here it is—a shameless hussy."

"It's all good publicity, Bill. If we can sell the public the idea that this is an immoral exhibition, we're sure to pack the house. That's why I wrote the letter."

"You mean you wrote it?"

"Sure—and the sporting editor was kind enough to see that it got published. Hot stuff, isn't it?"

"Bella, I'm ashamed of you."

"I'm not," said Bella. "But now I have a lot of other things to do. Good-bye." And Bella was gone.

On Saturday afternoon, the papers came out with more publicity, more objections, and an item stating that a member of the State Athletic Commission had decided to attend the bout in person. The Commissioner was quoted as saying that he stood—first, last and all the time—for good, clean sport. And there had been so much publicity and controversy about the coming bout, that he felt it his duty to make sure that everything was on the level and in accordance with the high moral standards heretofore always associated with the manly art of wrestling throughout the state.

Bill was considerably worried at the prospect of having the Athletic Commissioner at the bout. But Bella merely laughed: "All you have to do is follow my advice, and everything will be all right."

"I'm not so sure," said Bill.

"You're not losing your faith in me, are you?" asked Bella. "Don't you love me anymore?"

"Bella," said Bill, "you are the most wonderful woman in the world. You know I'm just crazy about you. Without you to handle things for me, I never would have amounted to anything. But this time I wish you would listen to me. It would be so much nicer to have just a simple quiet—"

"Bill," said Bella, "you're just too sweet for words, and I love you very much, and I just know you're going to carry this thing through the way I want you to."

"Well," said Bill, doubtfully. "If you insist—"

"Atta boy!" said Bella. She kissed him affectionately on his cheek just above the point where his beard began. "And now," she went on, briskly, "we've got to go down and see Clarence, and make the final arrangements."

Taking Bill by the hand, she led him down to the small Coliseum gymnasium, where Clarence Alford had just finished his afternoon workout. The term "Akron Adonis" fitted him fairly well. His face was rather weak and uninspiring, but his physical development was pretty much all right—broad shoulders, rippling muscles, and an undeniably graceful carriage. Bella motioned to Clarence. The three of them sat down on a bench, and Bella explained the details of the coming match.

"For the first ten or fifteen minutes," she said, "you guys can slam each other around in the usual way. But this is a very special occasion, so we ought to give the fans something new in the way of a finish. Here is the scenario: Clarence pulls a few flying tackles, maybe a couple of those phony flying handsprings, and Bill begins to act groggy. Then Clarence knocks Bill through the ropes, and Bill falls down in front of the first row of fans, and rolls in under the edge of the platform. Clarence stands looking down at the place where Bill disappeared and waiting for him to come back."

"There's nothing new about that," Clarence objected.

"Wait till you hear the rest," Bella said. "Instead of coming up where he went down, Bill creeps along under the platform and comes up into the ring on the far side. Clarence doesn't see him, because he has his back turned, and he's looking for him at the place where he disappeared. So Bill takes Clarence by surprise, slams him on the canvas, and wins the match. If you ask me, it's a good trick. The fans ought to eat it up."

"Yes, I guess it ought to work out all right," Bill admitted.

"But you want to be very careful, Bill," said Clarence, "when you hit me from behind. If you aren't careful you might hurt me."

"Don't you worry," Bill said. "I'll lay you down as gentle as if you were a crate of eggs."

"All right, then," Bella said. "It's settled. Now I have to go see about my wedding dress."

That was the last they saw of her until the evening performance.

When the doors were opened, there were already long lines of people waiting in the street. Sammy had boosted the prices, and the fans did a lot of grumbling, but they turned out just the same.

The last preliminary bout was over at half-past nine. The announcer then stepped up into the ring and explained that the grand entrance of the wedding party was about to take place. Afterward, the final bout would go on, and then the beautiful Miss Bella Jones would marry the winner.

As the announcer finished speaking, an orchestra arrived from the basement by means of the small stairway under the ring. The musicians climbed through the ropes, settled themselves on camp chairs, and started in on the well-known strains of *Oh Promise Me*. The words were sung by the announcer—amplified to a terrific roar by the public address system.

The fans, on the whole, did not like it. The lads in the cheap seats started a rhythmic stamping which almost drowned out the music. And the song ended in such a chorus of hoots and hisses that the announcer decided to skip *I Love You Truly*.

The orchestra swung into the opening bars of the *Lohengrin Wedding March*. A deep hush fell over the audience, accompanied by a great craning of necks as the wedding procession entered a rear door and moved down the aisle.

In front were two little flower girls—daughters of one of the preliminary wrestlers. They carried baskets of roses which they scattered before them as they advanced. There was some undignified scrambling around by nearby members of the audience who could not refrain from grabbing these roses as souvenirs. After the flower girls were six bridesmaids hired by a leading department store to model its latest gowns.

And then came Bella herself, a truly majestic figure in white satin, with a long veil. She leaned gracefully on the arm of Mr. Sammy Ringo, the promoter, who was beautifully dressed in full evening attire—including a white tie, white stiff shirt with large diamond studs, white satin vest, a coat with tails. Behind Bella were two little pages, sons of another wrestler, who carried her train.

The entire bridal party clambered into the ring, joined by the minister and the two bridegrooms, who came up from the basement. The timid-looking minister wore a dingy frock coat. The two bridegrooms were attired in wrestling trunks and bathrobes. Each was accompanied by a combination best man and second, clad in white pants and white sweater, and carrying a towel. The crowd burst into loud and enthusiastic applause. The announcer introduced the minister, the blushing bride, and the unhappy-looking bridegrooms. Then the orchestra disappeared into the basement. And the entire bridal party, with the exception of the two bridegrooms, climbed down into a section of the ringside seats which had been blocked off by white ribbon. Here also sat the Athletic Commissioner of the State.

The referee held his inevitable conference with the wrestlers. They removed their bathrobes, the big bell rang, and the great battle for the beautiful lady began.

Bill employed all his usual tricks for exciting the interest of the crowd. He expanded his vast hairy chest and beat upon it with his fists. He rumpled his hair and beard. He bared his teeth and growled and roared. And he went charging about the ring in his usual mad-bull fashion. Clarence employed the same Toreador[7] tactics which he had used in the past— gracefully side-stepping Bill's wild rushes, wiggling out of tight places, and occasionally closing in and taking a good pull at the heavy black beard of his opponent. From time to time the two men would grapple with each other and fall heavily. Bill would get an apparently effective hold and almost push Clarence's shoulders to the mat. And then, with a mighty heave, Clarence would wiggle loose and escape. It was a good show, and it had the fans roaring with delight.

Finally Clarence caught Bill off his guard and bounded off the ropes with a beautiful flying tackle that sent Bill sprawling. As Bill staggered to his feet, Clarence floored him with another tackle. Then Clarence pulled his most spectacular stunt—the flying handspring—striking Bill square in the chest with his feet, and knocking him backward into the ropes. As Bill dropped heavily over the edge and rolled in under the platform, the crowd leaped to its feet in a frenzy of excitement. Clarence waited, tense and expectant, just inside the ropes.

Slowly the referee began to count. According to the rules, if Bill failed to get back into the ring in twenty seconds he would lose the match. When the referee had reached the count of ten, he began to slow down. By the time he got to fifteen he was proceeding at about half the normal speed. And at sixteen he stopped entirely and began to look around in a puzzled sort of way.

The State Athletic Commissioner was on his feet. "You keep on counting," he shouted. "I'm here to see that this is a fair match!"

Reluctantly the referee took up his slow count.

Bella slid out of her seat, got down on her knees and peered under the platform. In the semi-darkness she was able to make out the vast form of Bill, partly hidden by the complicated network of criss-cross timbers which supported the platform. He had reached a point directly under the center of the ring.

---

7 **Toreador:** bullfighter

"Hey, there," Bella shouted. "You better hurry."

"I am," Bill answered. "But I'm caught. I seem to be wedged in between two of these timbers."

Bella went scuttling in under the platform—bridal veil and all. She crawled around, put her shoulder behind Bill and pushed.

Bill heaved and struggled until the entire platform swayed and shook. Then one of the timbers came loose with a crash, and Bill was on his way once more, with Bella right after him.

But it was too late. By the time he emerged at the side of the ring, the referee had reached the count of twenty, and the State Athletic Commissioner was shouting, "All right, what are you waiting for? Hold up the hand of the winner!"

The referee walked over and lifted Clarence's hand high in the air. The crowd was cheering and clapping and stamping. The little minister—thinking, no doubt, of the generous fee of twenty-five dollars which Bella had promised him—climbed eagerly into the ring. He opened his prayer book.

Down on the main floor beside the ring Bella spoke rapidly into Bill's ear. "I can't back out of this very well myself," she said. "So there's only one thing to do."

"What's that?" asked Bill.

"You've got to kidnap me by violence. Come on—pick me up and carry me out of here! And don't mind if I put up a fight. I got to stage a bit of a show for the benefit of the fans."

After a few seconds hesitation, Bill went into action. With one sweep of his mighty arm he swung the far-from-unsubstantial[8] form of his fiancée across his shoulders in a fireman's carry. But before he could start for the door he was diverted by a sudden commotion.

A large determined-looking woman came marching down the aisle. She reached the ring, climbed through the ropes, and walked over in front of Clarence.

"So this is what you are doing, you dirty little weasel!" she said in a shrill and angry voice. "Getting ready to commit bigamy[9]!"

"I can explain the whole thing," Clarence whined.

"I know all about it already," said the woman. "Apparently I was just in time. You can forget all about this new wedding, and from now on

8 **far-from-unsubstantial:** not small; large

9 **bigamy:** the act of marrying one person while still married to another

you're going to turn over all your spare cash to me, or I'll have you put in jail for non-support and desertion."

"Who are you?" asked the minister.

The lady pointed her finger at the cringing Clarence, and answered in a voice that came over the public address system like the roar of a Texas tornado: "I am this man's lawful wife!"

"Say," grunted Bella from her uncomfortable position across Bill's shoulders. "That's swell! It shows how far the publicity went; all the way to Newark, New Jersey. Now nobody can expect me to marry Clarence. So you can let me down, and you and I will get married according to the original plan."

"Bella," said Bill, "you got real brains. But I got the muscle."

"Put me down," yelled Bella.

"Shut up," said Bill. "I got you where I want you. And from now on I'm going to boss this affair."

He went up the aisle like a charging elephant. He carried the kicking and screaming Bella through the lobby, down to the dressing-rooms where he picked up his clothes, and out to the street where he hailed a passing taxi.

As they drove off, Bill braced himself for a terrific bawling out. But Bella merely gazed at him with love and admiration. "What a man!" she said. An hour later they were married by a minister in an outlying village. It was a simple, quiet wedding. ∽

Stealing for Girls

Will Weaver

It's a free country, right? I choose my clothes (sixties retro), I choose my shoes (Nikes), I choose my CDs (Hendrix and Nine Inch Nails), I choose my friends (you know who you are). If I were an adult (which I'm not—I'm a fourteen-year-old eighth-grade girl named Sun) I could vote, could choose my car, my career, whatever—like I said, a free country, right?

Wrong.

Quiz time: Please take out a number two lead pencil; *do not* open the test booklet until you're told. Seriously, my question to you is this: What's the most majorly thing in your life that you *can't* choose? The answer is as simple as the eyes and nose on your face: your parents. Your parents and your brothers or sisters. That's because no matter how free you think you are, the one thing nobody can choose for herself is her own family.

Here's another way of putting it: Being born is something like arriving at a restaurant where there are no waitrons and no menus. Your table is set and your food is there waiting for you. It might be fresh shrimp, it might be steak, it might be macaroni hot dish, it might be all broccoli; for some kids there might be no food at all, maybe not even a table.

Me? I was fairly lucky. My parents are (1) there, and (2) at least semi-cool most of the time. My dad's an accountant and my mom's a college professor. Both are in their middle forties, physically fit, and usually unembarrassing in public. My gripe is the old basic one for girls: My father spends way more time on sports with my brother, Luke, than with me.

Luke is in sixth grade, is already taller than me, and can pound me at basketball. At Ping-Pong. At any sport. You name it, he crushes me. I want to say right here I'm not a klutz. I'm nearly five feet six and have at least average coordination; on our basketball team I'm third off the bench, which is not that shabby considering that our school, Hawk Bend, is a basketball power in central Minnesota. But I won't play one-on-one with Luke anymore. No way. Who likes to lose every time? It's not like he's mean or wants to humiliate me—he's actually pretty decent for a twerpy sixth-grade boy—it's just that he's a natural athlete and I'm not.

I am thinking these thoughts as I sit next to my parents watching Luke's team play Wheatville. Luke just made a nifty spin move (of course, he's the starting point guard)[1] and drove the lane for a layup. My mother, who comes to most games, stares at Luke with her usual astounded look. She murmurs to my father, who comes to all our games, "How did he do that?"

"Head fake right, plant pivot foot, big swing with leading leg, and bingo—he's by," my dad whispers. A quiet but intense man with salt-and-pepper hair, he speaks from the side of his mouth, for there are always parents of other sixth-graders nearby.

"He amazes me," my mother says. She has not taken her eyes off Luke. I hate to agree, but she's right—all of which clouds further my normally "sunny" disposition. I remember Dad and Luke working last winter on that very move in the basement; I went downstairs to see what was going on, and they both looked up at me like I was an alien from the *Weekly World News*. My father soon enough bounced the ball to me, and I gave it a try, but I could never get my spin dribble to rotate quickly

1 **point guard:** the player on a basketball team who is responsible for running the offense

enough and in a straight line forward to the basket. Not like you-know-who. "Watch Luke," my father said. "He'll demonstrate."

Now, at least it's the third quarter of the game and Luke already has a lot of points and his team is ahead by twenty so the coach will take him out soon—though not quite soon enough for Wheatville, or me. At the other end of the court Luke's loose, skinny-legged body and flopping yellow hair darts forward like a stroke of heat lightning to deflect the ball.

"Go, Luke!" my father says, half rising from his seat.

Luke is already gone, gathering up the ball on a break-away, finishing with a soft layup high off the board. People clap wildly.

I clap slowly. Briefly. Politely. My mother just shakes her head. "How does he *do* that?"

"Ask *him*," I mutter.

"Pardon, Sun?" my mom says abstractedly.

"Nothing." I check the scoreboard, then my own watch. I've seen enough. Below, at floor level, some friends are passing. "I think I'll go hang with Tara and Rochelle," I say to my parents.

"Sure," my mother says vacantly.

Dad doesn't hear me or see me leave.

As I clump down the bleachers there is more cheering, but I prefer not to look. "Sun." What a stupid name—and by the way I do not *ever* answer to "Sunny." I was allegedly born on a Sunday, on a day when the sun was particularly bright, or so my parents maintain. I seriously doubt their version (someday I'm going to look up the actual weather report on March 18, 1980). I'm sure it was a Monday; either that or I was switched at the hospital. Or maybe it was Luke—one of us, definitely, was switched.

Rochelle, actually looking once or twice at the game, says right off, "Say, wasn't that your little brother?"

"I have no brother," I mutter.

"He's a smooth little dude," Tara says, glancing over her shoulder. "Kinda cute, actually."

"Can I have some popcorn or what?" I say.

"Or what," Rochelle says, covering her bag.

They giggle hysterically. Real comediennes, these two.

"When's your next game?" Tara says to me, relenting, giving me three whole kernels.

"The last one is Tuesday night," I answer. "A makeup game with Big Falls."

"Here or away?"

"Here."

"With your record, maybe you could get your little brother to play for your team."

"Yeah—a little eye shadow, a training bra," adds Rochelle, "everyone would think he was you!"

I growl something unprintable to my friends and go buy my own bag of popcorn.

▲ ▲ ▲

At supper that night Luke and I stare at each other during grace, our usual game—see who will blink first. Tonight it is me. I glare down at my broccoli and fish; I can feel him grinning.

"And thank you, God, for bouncing the ball our way once again," my father finishes. "Amen." If God doesn't understand sports metaphors, our family is in huge trouble.

"Well," my father says, looking at Luke expectantly.

"A deep subject," Luke says automatically, reaching for his milk, automatically.

Both of them are trying not to be the first one to talk about the game.

"How was your day, Sun?" my mother says.

"I hate it when you do that."

"Do what?" my mother says.

"It's condescending," I add.

"What is condescending?" she protests.

"Asking me about my day when the thing on everybody's mind is Luke's usual great game. Why not just say it: 'So, Luke, what were the numbers?' "

There is silence; I see Luke cast an uncertain glance toward my father.

"That's not at all what I meant," Mother says.

"And watch that tone of voice," my father warns me.

"So how many points *did* you get?" I say to Luke, clanking the broccoli spoon back into the dish, holding the dish in front of his face; he hates broccoli.

He shrugs, mumbles, "Not sure, really."

"How many?" I press.

"I dunno. Fifteen or so." But he can't help himself: He bites his lip, tries to scowl, fakes a cough, but the smile is too strong.

"How *many*?" I demand.

"Maybe it was twenty," he murmurs.

I pick up a large clump of broccoli and aim it at his head.

"Sun!" my father exclaims.

Luke's eyes widen. "Twenty-six!" he squeaks.

"There. That wasn't so difficult, was it?" I say, biting the head off the broccoli.

Luke lets out a breath, begins to eat. There is a silence for a while.

"By the way—nice steal there at the end," I say to him as I pass the fish to Father.

Luke looks up at me from the top of his eyes. "Thanks," he says warily.

"It's something I should work on," I add.

"I'll help you!" Luke says instantly and sincerely. "Right after supper!"

At this syrupy sibling exchange, my parents relax and dinner proceeds smoothly.

Later, during dessert, when my father and Luke have finally debriefed themselves—quarter by quarter, play by play—on the game, I wait for Dad's usual "Well, who's next on the schedule, Luke?" He doesn't disappoint me.

"Clearville, I think," Luke says.

"Any breakdown on them? Stats?"

"They're eight-four on the season, have that big center who puts up *numbers*, plus a smooth point guard. They beat us by six last time," Luke says. My mind skips ahead twenty years and sees Luke with his own accounting office, crunching tax returns by day and shooting hoops long into the evening.

"Big game, then, yes?" my father remarks, his fingers beginning to drum on the table. "You'll have to box out—keep that big guy off the boards. And if their point guard penetrates, collapse inside—make him prove he can hit the jumper."

"He can't hit no jumpers," Luke says through a large bite of cake. "He shoots bricks, and I'm going to shut him down like a bike lock."

"Huh?" I say.

"What?" Luke says. "What'd I say now?"

"First off, it's 'any jumper.' And second, how do you shut someone down 'like a bike lock'?"

"Actually, it's not a bad simile," my mother says. "If this fellow is 'smooth,' so, in a way, is a bicycle—the way it rolls and turns—and a bike lock, well . . ." She trails off, looking at me.

I shrug and stare down at my fish. It has not been a good day for either of us.

"And who does *your* team play next, Sun?" my father asks dutifully.

"Big Falls. Tuesday night," I say. I look up and watch his face carefully.

"Tuesday night, isn't that? . . ." he begins.

"I'm afraid I'll miss it, honey," my mother interjects. "I have that teachers' education conference in Minneapolis, remember?"

"Sure, Mom, no problem." I keep my eyes on my father; on Luke, who's thinking. I am waiting for the lightbulb (twenty watts, maximum) to go on in his brain.

"Hey—Tuesday night is my game, too," Luke says suddenly.

"Yes, I thought so," my father murmurs. The one-on-one experts have finally put two and two together.

"What time are your games?" my mother asks.

"Seven," Luke and I say simultaneously.

My father looks to me, then to Luke. He's frowning. Suddenly his gaze lightens. "By any chance are they both at the high school? In the adjoining gyms?"

"Middle school," Luke says.

"High school," I follow.

"Darn," my father says, "they ought to take whoever schedules sporting events in this school system and—"

"I'm sure it couldn't be helped, dear," my mother interjects. "Sun's is a makeup game, after all."

"And the last one of the season," I add.

My father looks to Luke. "So is yours, right? The last one of the season?"

Luke nods. He and I look at each other. I smile. I love moral dilemmas, especially when they're not mine.

My father turns to my mother.

"Sorry," she says to him, "I'm delivering a speech in Minneapolis. There's no way I can miss it."

"Well," my father says, drumming his fingers, "I'll have to think this one through."

▲ ▲ ▲

Amazingly, Luke keeps his promise, and after dinner we work on stealing. It is chilly outside in March, with patches of leftover snowbanks along the north side of the garage (this is Minnesota, remember), but the asphalt is clear.

"There are two main types of steals," Luke says, dribbling. "First is the most basic, 'the unprotected ball.' As your man is dribbling, he is not shielding the ball with his body, and so you go for it."

"I have part of a brain," I say, and lunge for the deflection—but Luke instantly back-dribbles, and I miss.

"It's all in the timing," he says, "all in when you start your move. Don't start when the ball is coming back up to my hand—begin your move just when the ball *leaves* my hand, just when it's released and heading downward."

I track him, waiting—then try it. This time I actually knock the ball away.

"See?" Luke says. "That gives you the maximum time for your reach-in."

We practice this a few more times.

"Be sure to reach with your outside hand," Luke cautions, "or else you might get called for a reach-in foul."

We keep working for quite a while. I start to get every third one, but I'm still not very good at it.

"It's coming," Luke says, then holds the ball. I kick away a pebble, which clatters against the garage door.

"The second type of steal is called the wraparound. It's when your man is dribbling and you reach way around behind, almost wrapping your arm around him, and knock the ball away." He flips me the ball, has me dribble, and snakes loose the ball two out of three times. Then he takes the ball back, and we work on this one for a while. I get one out of ten at best. Soon I am panting.

"The wraparound is the toughest one," Luke says. "Maybe you need longer arms or something."

From the window, my father is watching us. "Again," I say crabbily to Luke. Soon I am stumbling-tired and getting no wraparound deflections or steals at all.

"Hey—it'll come," Luke says, bouncing the ball to me. I slam the ball hard onto the cold asphalt and back into my hands.

"Yeah. Like in 2010 maybe," I say, then mutter something unprintable.

"Ah . . . I think I'll go have some more cake," Luke says.

"Fine!" I bark. He heads off.

"By the way," I call after him, "who taught you those stealing moves?" The middle-school coaches teach both the girls' and boys' teams, and I am always on the lookout for coaches who treat boys and girls differently. Nothing annoys me more than that.

"Who taught me? Coach Dad," Luke says with an innocent smile.

I don't smile. I glare at Luke, then to the window, which is empty.

"What?" Luke says, glancing behind. "What did I say now?"

"Nothing." I turn away, take the ball, and begin to bank hard shots off the backboard, none of which fall.

▲   ▲   ▲

That night, as my father sits at the kitchen table rattling his calculator keys and turning the pages of someone's tax return (from March through

April 15 we leave him alone), I find myself rattling the dishes hard and loud as I clean up the kitchen.

"Was there something? . . ." he says irritatedly, glancing up only briefly from his papers.

"No," I say, and stomp past him upstairs to my room.

Later I hear my mother speaking softly to my father. He lets out a sigh and pushes back from the table. Soon I hear his footsteps on the stairs, and then he pops his head partway into my room, where I am reading. "Everything okay, Sun?"

"Sure," I mutter.

"Sure sure?"

I shrug.

He leans in my doorway. "So what is it?" he asks, checking his watch.

"How come you taught Luke those two types of steals and not me?" I turn to him. My eyes, disgustingly, feel glassy and spilly; they are about to dump water down my cheeks.

He stares. "Steals? Oh, you mean . . . Yes, well . . ." He trails off and stares at some empty space in front of him, thinking. Then he turns to me. "I guess I just naturally do more sports stuff with Luke because . . . because we're both boys—I mean I once was, and he's one now, that sort of thing," he finishes lamely.

"Well, I play basketball, too," I say. I try to be hard-boiled but a large tear rolls down my cheek. "Darn," I blurt, and start crying for real.

He stares at me, then moves imperceptibly, as if to come forward either to smack me or to take me in his arms. But accountants are accountants because most of them are not good with other things—like feelings. With a confused look on his face, my father retreats from my room.

In the morning when I wake up, there is a note taped to my door. In his small, careful handwriting my father has written, "Dear Sun: There is a third type of steal. . . ."

▲ ▲ ▲

That Saturday, when Luke is gone to hockey, my father appears in the TV room wearing his tennis shoes and sweats. "'Stealing for Girls,' a sports clinic by yours truly, begins in fifteen minutes, garage-side."

I smile, grab the remote, and shoot the TV dead.

Before we go outside, my father sits at the kitchen table and begins drawing neat *X*'s and *O*'s on graph paper. "We'll call this third type the prediction pass steal. It's something that works best with a zone defense."[2]

"Okay," I say. On my team we have been learning the zone, and zone traps, though we haven't used them much.

"A half-court zone defense forces the team on offense to work the ball around the perimeter."

I nod as he draws lines in a large half circle.

"The faster the ball movement, the tougher it is for the defense to shift accordingly."

I nod. I know all this.

"The offensive point guard will sooner or later get into what you might call the automatic pass mode—he receives a pass from, say, his right side, and automatically turns to pass to his left."

"Yeah, sure," I murmur, for I am thinking of something that has always puzzled me.

"What is it?" my father asks with a trace of impatience.

"If you never played basketball in high school or college, how come you know so much about the game?"

He looks up straight at me. There is a long moment of silence. "I would like to have played," he says simply, "but it was a big school."

I meet his gaze, then put my hand on his shoulder.

He smiles, a small but real smile, and we both turn back to the graph paper.

"Anyway, when the point guard gets sloppy," he continues, "that's when the smart defensive man can start to think about a prediction pass steal."

"The defensive point guard?"

"No," my father says immediately. "The offensive point guard is used to that; he's been conditioned to watch out for that kind of steal. What he's not expecting is the weak-side defensive guard or even the forward to break up and across, slanting through the lane toward the key and picking off the pass. A lot of the quick but small college teams use it."

"Show me," I say, staring down at the paper.

He grabs a fresh graph. "Imagine a basic zone defense that's shifting to the ball."

I close my eyes. "Got it," I say.

2 **zone defense:** a game plan where each player guards a specified area of the court instead of a specific opponent

"If the offense is moving the ball sharply, the defensive point guard has the toughest job. He usually can't keep up with the ball movement."

I nod. I keep my eyes closed.

"So the passes out front become 'gimmes'; they're not contested."

I nod again.

"And after a while, the offensive point guard gets sloppy. That's when one of the defensive players down low—the forward or center—can make his move. He flashes all the way up, comes out of nowhere for the steal."

My smile opens my eyes.

"Keep in mind it will only work once or twice," my father cautions, "and the timing has to be perfect—or the defense will get burned."

I look down to his drawing, see the open hole left by the steal attempt.

"Burned bad," he adds. "But if it works—bingo—he's gone for an easy layup."

I correct him: "*She's* gone."

▲   ▲   ▲

Outside, for want of five offensive players, my father presses into service a sawhorse, three garbage cans, and my mother. "I just love my team," she says wryly.

"This won't take long," my dad says. Mom shivers; the weather is cloudy, with rain forecast.

"Sun, you're the weak-side defensive guard," he directs. I position myself, back to the basket. "Honey, you're our offensive point guard," he says to my mother.

"I've never been a point guard; I've never been a guard of any kind," she protests.

"First time for everything," my dad retorts.

Actually, I can tell that they're both having at least a little fun.

"Now," he says to my mom, "imagine you have just received a pass from the sawhorse, and in turn you'll be passing to me."

My mother, the orange ball looking very large in her hands, says, "Thanks—sawhorse," and turns and passes to my dad.

"Now—Sun!" he calls, but I break up way too late.

"Again," my father says.

This time I break up too soon, and my mother stops her pass.

"Again," my father says.

I trot back to my position and try it again. On the sixth try I time it perfectly: I catch her pass chest-high and am gone for an imaginary layup.

"Excellent!" my father calls. "Again."

We practice until we are glowing in the chilly March morning, until an icy rain starts spattering down and the ball becomes too slick to hold.

Afterward, we are sitting at the kitchen table drinking hot chocolate when outside a car door slams—Luke's ride—and then Luke thumps into the house. "Hey," he says, pointing over his shoulder, "what's with the garbage cans and the sawhorse?"

The three of us look at each other; I smile and say nothing.

▲   ▲   ▲

For the next several days, my father and I work exactly forty-five minutes per evening on the prediction pass steal. I let Luke join us only because we need another passer. The weather remains lousy, and my mother freezes her butt off, and Luke complains about not getting to try the prediction steal himself, but my father ignores all that. He is too busy fine-tuning my timing, my breakaways.

And, suddenly, it is Tuesday morning of game day.

Both games.

"Huge day—two big games," my father says, first thing, at breakfast. He drums his fingers, glances at his briefcase, at the clock.

Luke glares at me. He is not happy about this week and his role as perpetual passer. "I guess I know which game you're going to," he mutters to my father.

My father says nothing.

▲   ▲   ▲

Warming up with the team, I have the usual butterflies. The Big Falls girls look like their name—big, with huge hair tied back and bouncing like waterfalls as they do their layups. I try not to look at them, but can't help but hear their chatter, the chirp and thud of their shoes. Even their feet are huge.

I look around the gym. No family. No Dad. I miss my layup.

Just before tip-off, from my spot on the bench, I look around one last time. No family. No father. I sigh and try to focus on the game.

Which is going to be a tough one all the way. The teams are well matched at every position, and we trade basket for basket—bad news for me. I ride the pine all the way through the first quarter.

We do our "Hawk Bend Fliers!" send-off whoop to start the second quarter, and as I head back to the bench I scan the small crowd. Still no father. But it's just as well, I think gloomily as I settle onto the bench—at least at Luke's game he's seeing Luke play. Logically, if I were a parent I wouldn't come to my game, either.

Watching, chin in hands, that second quarter, with a sparse, quiet crowd giving neither team much support, I begin to think dark but true thoughts: that really, in the end, each of is alone. That each of us, by what we choose to do, is responsible for what we achieve and how we feel about ourselves. That each of us—

"Sun. Sun!" An elbow, Jenny's, jabs me in the ribs: The coach is calling for me.

"Sun, check in for Rachel," Coach Brown says, then adds, "At forward," giving me a fleeting, get-your-head-in-the-game glance.

I have to ask Rachel who she's guarding. Tired, irritated at having to pause on her way off the floor, she looks around and finally points to a hefty, five-foot-ten forward with major pimples on her shoulders and neck. I trot up close.

"What are you staring at?" the sweaty Big Falls forward says straight off. Then she leans close to me and glares.

"There's a new soap that might clear those up," I say, letting my eyes fall to her neck and shoulders.

"Listen, you little —" she says, but the horn drowns out the rest.

Then the ball is in play. It comes quickly to my man, who puts her shoulder down and drives the lane. I keep my feet planted and draw the charging foul.

"Way to go, Sun," my team calls as we head up the floor, and my mood lightens considerably.

In my two minutes of play I make one lucky basket and draw one foul— a reach-in steal attempt. I try to remember that timing is everything. I also see that our team is quicker, but Big Falls is stronger inside. Pimple Shoulders muscles me out of the way for an easy bank shot, like I was a mosquito on an alligator's back. She outweighs me by eighty pounds, minimum.

At the next time-out Rachel comes back in and I end up sitting next to the coach. I watch us get beat inside by some teeth-jarring picks and back screens;[3] the score gradually tilts in favor of Big Falls. At the half we are down 28–21.

---

3 **picks and back screens:** an offensive strategy where a teammate of the player with the ball blocks the path of the opposing team's defender so the ball handler can attempt to get open to make a pass or a shot.

▲ ▲ ▲

In the locker room the first five players lie red-faced and flat on their backs on the benches. "They're shoving underneath," Rachel complains.

"No—they're outmuscling us," Coach retorts. "Position! We've got to get position and stay planted. Like Sun did right away when she came in—get planted and draw the foul."

I play it very cool and do not change expressions.

The coach heads to the chalkboard and begins to draw X's and O's. "They might be big, but they're slow. In the third quarter I want us to run, run, run—fast-break them until their butts are dragging."

"Or ours," Rachel mutters.

"You don't want to play hard, we've got people who do!" Coach barks. Rachel zips her lips, stares at the ceiling.

▲ ▲ ▲

During the halftime shoot I scan the crowd. Still nobody. I feel something inside me harden further, and center itself; it's a flash of what life will be like when I go away to college, when I'll truly be on my own. Just me. No family whatsoever. Just me shlumping along through life.

On the bench as the third quarter begins, for some reason I finally get focused. I sit next to the coach; I chatter out encouragement. Our fast break begins to work. After they score or we get a rebound, Rachel rips the ball to one side or the other while Jenny, our point guard, breaks up the center. She takes the pass at the half-court line, then does her thing—either driving the lane or dishing off to the trailers.[4] We miss some easy layups but still pull within one point.

Big Falls calls time-out. Our subs are ecstatic,[5] but the starting five stand bent over, hands on knees, wheezing.

"Let's try to keep the fast break working through the end of this quarter," Coach Brown says, "and then we'll figure out something else."

Our starters manage a weak "Go Fliers" and trudge back onto the floor.

In the final two minutes of the third quarter I watch as Big Falls shuts down the fast break like . . . like a bicycle lock. Simple, really—just some pressure on the out-of-bounds first pass, plus coverage on the sides—and we do not score again. But I have been watching them on offense. Nearly every time down the court, Pimple Shoulders rears up inside, then looks

4 **dishing off to the trailers:** passing the ball to teammates coming downcourt behind her

5 **ecstatic:** thrilled

for the pass from the point guard—who has taken very few shots from the perimeter, including zero three-point attempts.

"Zone," I say to myself. "In the fourth quarter we should go zone."

Coach Brown looks to me. Then back to the action. He strokes his chin.

At the final quarter break he kneels on the floor. "Take a load off," he commands, and the starting five slump into chairs. He points, one by one, to the next five, and we check in. Back in the huddle, Coach Brown has drawn some scrawling maps of *X*'s and *O*'s. "Zone defense," he says, with a wink to me. "Let's collapse inside and make them shoot from the perimeter. Make them prove they can hit the jumpers. But box out and get that rebound," he adds. "We've got to have the ball to score."

We fire up and trot onto the floor. For some reason I look to the middle of the bleachers—and see my father. His brief-case rests beside him and his gray suit coat is folded neatly over it.

"Zone! Box and one!" the Big Falls point guard calls out immediately, and begins to move the ball crisply side to front to side. It's clear they've had a zone thrown at them before. Still bench-stiff, we have trouble keeping up with the passes, and their point guard takes an uncontested shot from within the key—but bricks it.[6] Wendy rips off the rebound and we move the ball cautiously upcourt. Our second-team guards have no future with the Harlem Globetrotters in terms of ballhandling, but we do know how to pick-and-roll.[7]

I fake to the baseline, then break up and set a screen for Shanna. She rubs off her girl—who hits me, blindside, hard—as I roll to the inside. I'm

6 **bricks it:** completely misses

7 **pick-and-roll:** an offensive strategy that takes place near the baseline when a teammate of the ball handler stands behind the opposing team's defender and blocks the defenders's path so that the ball handler can drive to make basket or pass to the teammate who has rolled to the basket after blocking the defender.

looking for the ball, and suddenly, thanks to a nifty bounce pass, it's right at my chest. I clamp on it, take one dribble, brace for a hammer blow from Pimple Shoulders, and go up for the lay-in. I feel the oncoming air rush of a large-body (the image of a 747 jetliner on a crash course with a seagull flashes through my mind) but don't alter my flight path. The ball feels good off my fingertips. As my feet touch down and I open my eyes, the ball is settling through the net and Pimple Shoulders is skidding along the hardwood runway and there is major cheering from our bench. Me? I am just happy to be heading upcourt with all my feathers intact.

The Big Falls outside shooting continues to bang hard off the rim, and we continue to box out and get the rebound play and score on basic pick-and-rolls. We go up 42–38, and our bench is screaming and bouncing up and down in their chairs.

But Big Falls gets smart: They throw a zone defense at us. Not great passers, and worse outside shooters, we turn the ball over three times; barely fifty seconds later, Big Falls is up by two, 44–42, and Coach Brown is screaming for a time-out. By the time the ref stops the clock there is less than three minutes left in the game.

"Okay, good job, second team," he calls, pointing for the first team to check back in. "Stay with the zone defense, but let's run the fast break."

We all clap once, together, and send the starters back onto the floor.

"Nice work out there," the coach says to me, and motions for me to sit by him. "Stay ready."

The first team, refreshed, runs a fast break for a quick bucket and knots the score at 44 all. The teams trade baskets, then settle into solid defense, and suddenly there is less than one minute to play. Both the score and my gut are knotted. The Big Falls point guard launches a three-pointer, which goes through, but we come back with a fast break on which Rachel does some kind of wild, falling, 180-degree, dipsy-do finger-roll shot—which falls! We are down by one point, but Rachel is down, too, with a turned ankle. There are thirty seconds left.

We help her off the court. Done for the day, she cries with pain and anger.

"Sun—check in and go to forward," the coach says.

As I pause at the scorer's table, everything seems exaggeratedly clear, as if magnified: the black and white zebra stripes of the officials, the seams of the yellow wood floor, the orange rim worn to bare, shiny metal on the inside. I stare at the ball the ref is holding and can imagine its warm, tight sphere in my hands. I want that ball. For the first time in my basketball career I want the ball, bad.

The Big Falls girls are slapping high fives like the game is over; after all, they have possession with a one-point lead. The ref calls time-in, and Big Falls bounces the ball inbounds handily and pushes it quickly up the floor. There they spread the offense and begin to work the ball around the perimeter: side to front to side to front. It's too early for us to foul, so we stay with our zone defense. Their point guard, still jazzed from making the three-point basket, is loose and smart-mouthed. As she receives the ball she automatically passes it to the opposite side.

Which is when I suddenly see not Big Falls players but garbage cans and a sawhorse. To the side, on the bench, I see Coach Brown rising to signal it's time to foul, but I have been counting off another kind of time: the Big Falls passing rhythm. On the far side, away from the ball, when orange is flashing halfway to the point guard, I begin my break. Smart Mouth receives the ball, turns, and passes it. Her eyes bug out as I arrow into view; she tries to halt her pass but it's too late. I catch the ball and am gone. There is only open floor in front and sudden cheering from the sides, and, overly excited, I launch my layup at about the free throw line—but the ball goes in anyway. The Hawk Bend crowd goes crazy.

Down by one point, Big Falls calls a frantic time-out at the five-second mark. Our players are delirious, but Coach Brown is not. "Watch for the long pass, the long pass!" he rants. "They have a set play. Don't foul—especially on the three-point shot."

But we're only eighth-graders; at times we don't listen well.

Sure enough, Big Falls screens on the inbound pass, which Pimple Shoulders fires full court. There the point guard takes an off-balance shot—and is fouled by Shanna as time runs out.

Shanna looks paralyzed. She can't believe she did it.

"Three-point attempt—three foul shots!" the ref calls.

We clear off the free throw line and watch her make the first two—to tie—and miss the third. The game goes into overtime.

Back in the huddle we try to get pumped again, but I can tell it's not going to happen. We are stunned and flat. We lose in overtime by four points.

▲　▲　▲

Back home we have a late supper: broccoli, fish sticks, and rice. I stare at my plate as my father finishes grace. Then he looks up. "Well," he says.

"A very deep subject," Luke replies, grabbing the bread. His team won, of course, by twenty-six points.

I just sit there, slumped and staring.

"You should have seen it," my father begins, speaking to Luke. "We're down by one and your sister is low on the weak side. The Big Falls point guard is not paying attention. . . ." Slowly I look up. I listen as my father tells the story of my one and only career steal. He re-creates it so well that Luke stops eating and his mouth drops open slightly. "Rad!" Luke says at the finish, then asks me more about my game. I shrug, but end up giving him a virtual play-by-play of the last two minutes.

When I am done, Luke lets out a breath and looks squarely at me. "Wow—I wish I could have been there!"

I stop to stare at him.

"What—what'd I say?" Luke says warily.

I just smile, and pass my little brother the broccoli. ❧

RESPONDING TO CLUSTER FOUR

THINKING ON YOUR OWN
Thinking Skill SYNTHESIZING

1. Each of the other clusters in this book is introduced by a question that is meant to help readers focus their thinking about the selections. What do you think the question for cluster four should be?

2. How do you think the selections in this cluster should be taught? Demonstrate your ideas by joining with your classmates to do one or more of the following.

   a. create discussion questions

   b. lead discussions about the selections

   c. develop vocabulary activities

   d. prepare a cluster quiz

REFLECTING ON *THE MAIN EVENT*
Essential Question WHAT IS THE VALUE OF SPORT?

Reflecting on this book as a whole provides an opportunity for independent learning and the application of the critical thinking skill, synthesis. *Synthesizing* means examining all the things you have learned from this book and combining them to form a richer and more meaningful view of why people play and watch sports.

There are many ways to demonstrate what you know about the value of sport. Here are some possibilities. Your teacher may provide others.

1. Some people are passionate fans of one sport, yet cannot understand why anyone would want to watch another sport. Using the information in the selections and your own experiences, write a persuasive essay to convince another person to become a fan of your favorite sport. As you write your essay, keep in mind the essential question stated above.

2. Individually or in small groups, develop an independent project that demonstrates your knowledge of a sport, sports history, or another perspectives on sports. For example, you might create your own TV sports show or stage a debate on the question "Do schools give too much time, money, and importance to sports?" Other options might include music, dance, poetry, a dramatic performance, or an artistic rendering.

ACKNOWLEDGMENTS

Text Credits CONTINUED FROM PAGE 2 "Joan Benoit," poem by Rina Ferrarelli from *American Sports Poems* (Orchard, 1988). Copyright © 1986 by Rina Ferrarelli. Reprinted by permission of the author.

"Just Once" by Thomas J. Dygard, from *Ultimate Sports* by Donald R. Gallo. Copyright © 1995 by Donald R. Gallo. Used by permission of Random House Children's Books, a division of Random House, Inc.

"Nine Triads" from *The Sidewalk Racer and Other Poems of Sports and Motion* by Lillian Morrison. Copyright © 1965, 1967, 1968, 1977 by Lillian Morrison. Used by permission of Marian Reiner for the author.

"The Noble Experiment" from *I Never Had It Made* by Jackie Robinson, as told to Alfred Duckett. TM/© 1999 Rachel Robinson licensed by CMG Worldwide Inc., Indianapolis, IN 46256, www.cmgww.com.

"Olympics in Ancient Greece" from *Olympism* by Griffin Publishing. Copyright © 1996 by Griffin Publishing. Reprinted by permission of Griffin Publishing, 2908 Oregon Court, Suite I-5, Torrance, CA 90503, 800-472-9741, www. griffinpublishing.com.

"A Quiet Wedding" by William Hazlett Upson. First published in *Esquire* magazine. All rights reserved. Copyright © 1941 by William Hazlett Upson. Copyright renewed © 1968 by William Hazlett Upson. Reprinted by permission of Brandt & Brandt Literary Agents, Inc.

Reprinted from *Seen and Heard*; photographs and text copyright © 1998 Mary Motley Kalergis. Permission granted by Stewart, Tabori & Chang Publishers, New York.

"Stealing for Girls" by Will Weaver, from *Ultimate Sports* by Donald R. Gallo. Copyright © 1995 by Donald R. Gallo. Used by permission of Random House Children's Books, a division of Random House, Inc.

"This Girl Gets Her Kicks" by Rick Reilly. Reprinted courtesy of *Sports Illustrated* magazine, October 19, 1998. Copyright © 1998 Time, Inc. All rights reserved.

"Unsportsman-like Conduct" by Dave Barry. Copyright © 1983 by Dave Barry. Reprinted by permission of the author.

"Walking Away While He Still Can" by Ira Berkow, from *The New York Times*, January 1, 1993. Copyright © 1993 by The New York Times. Reprinted by permission.

"Watching Gymnasts" from *Collected Poems: 1936-1976* by Robert Francis (Amherst: University of Massachusetts Press, 1976). Copyright © 1961 by Robert Francis. Reprinted by permission of The University of Massachusetts Press.

"When the Boys Taught Their Coach" by Richard Alan Nesbitt. Reprinted with permission from the August 1996 *Reader's Digest*. Copyright © 1996 by The Reader's Digest Assn., Inc.

"White Men Can Jump" by Dan Cray from *Time* magazine, December 14, 1998. Copyright © 1998 Time, Inc. Reprinted by permission.

Every reasonable effort has been made to properly acknowledge ownership of all material used. Any omissions or mistakes are not intentional and, if brought to the publisher's attention, will be corrected in future editions.

Photo and Art Credits Cover and Title Page: Jim Tsinganos, *Beach Scene*. Pages 4-5: ©1997 R. Nakagawa/Photonica. Page 11: TL, William Sallaz/Duomo; TR, AP/Wide World Photos; BL, ©1998 Steven E. Sutton/Duomo; BR, AP/Wide World Photos. Page 12: TL, Allsport/©Hulton Deutsch; TR, AP/Wide World Photos; BL, ©Allsport/Hulton Deutsch; BR, AP/Wide World Photos. Page 12: TL, Allsport/©Hulton Deutsch; TR, AP/Wide World Photos; BL, ©Allsport/Hulton Deutsch; BR, AP/Wide World Photos. Page 13: TL, ©1997 William Sallaz/Duomo; BL, ©1991 Duomo; BR, ©Allsport/Hulton Getty. Page 15: ©Robin M. White/Photonica. Page 16: ©Pedro Lobo/Photonica. Page 25: ©John Still/Photonica. Page 26: ©1994 William Sallaz/Duomo. Page 27: ©1987 Steven E. Sutton/Duomo. Pages 28-29: John Huet. Page 31: ©1998 Mitchell Layton/Duomo. Page 34: Myron of Athens, (5th c. BCE) *Discobolus*, Roman copy of Greek original (c. 450 BCE) Museo Nazionale Romano delle Terme, Rome, Italy. Scala/Art Resource, NY. Page 37: 35.21 *Demareteion*, silver coin. Theodora Wilbour Fund in memory of Zöe Wilbour. Museum of Fine Arts, Boston. Pages 38-39: *Young Men Wrestling*, marble relief from a statue base found in the Dipylon cemetery, Athens, c. 510 BC. National Archaeological Museum, Athens, Greece. Bridgeman Art Library, London/New York. Page 41: 21.1194 *Kneeling Archer*, gem, chalcedony, c. 500 BC. Francis Bartlett Fund, Museum of Fine Arts, Boston. Page 43: John P. Kelly/Image Bank. Page 45: Ahmad Terry/Rocky Mountain News. Page 46: Rick Rickman. Page 49: ©Tony Duffy/Allsport. Pages 50-51: ©Jake Wyman/Photonica. Pages 54-55 Hussey & Hussey/Image Bank. Page 58: Wayne Thiebaud, *Football Player*, 1963. Oil on canvas, 72"H. x 36"W, Virginia Museum of Fine Arts, Richmond. Gift of the Sydney and Frances Lewis Foundation. ©Virginia Museum of Fine Arts. Page 65: ©Henry Horenstein/Photonica. Page 67 Yellow Dog Productions/Image Bank. Page 68: AP/Wide World Photos. Page 78: Larry Zingale, *Somebody's Grandmother*, 1982. Oil on canvas. Pages 88, 91, 95: AP/Wide World Photos. Page 99: ©1990 Mitchell Layton/Duomo. Page 103: ©1990 Al Tielemana/Duomo. Page 105: ©John C. Russeli/Phototonica. Page 107, 108: ©Mary Motley Kalergis. Pages 114, 124: Seymour Chwast. Page 125: ©1997 Tom Maday/Photonica. Page 131: Index Stock Imagery. Page 139: ©Henry Horenstein/Photonica.